The Law of the Parish Church

PREVIOUS EDITIONS

First Edition (with Foreword by Lord Atkin)	1932
Second Edition	1946
Third Edition	1957
Fourth Edition	1967
Fifth Edition	1975

The Law of the Parish Church

*An account of the powers, rights and
duties of the Incumbent, the Churchwardens,
the Parochial Church Council
and the Parishioners*

SIR WILLIAM DALE, K.C.M.G.

of Gray's Inn and Lincoln's Inn, Barrister

SIXTH EDITION

BUTTERWORTHS
LONDON
1989

United Kingdom	Butterworth & Co (Publishers) Ltd, 88 Kingsway, LONDON WC2B 6AB and 4 Hill Street, EDINBURGH EH2 3JZ
Australia	Butterworths Pty Ltd, SYDNEY, MELBOURNE, BRISBANE, ADELAIDE, PERTH, CANBERRA and HOBART
Canada	Butterworths Canada Ltd, TORONTO and VANCOUVER
Ireland	Butterworth (Ireland) Ltd, DUBLIN
New Zealand	Butterworths of New Zealand Ltd, WELLINGTON and AUCKLAND
Puerto Rico	Equity de Puerto Rico, Inc, HATO REY
Singapore	Malayan Law Journal Pte Ltd, SINGAPORE
USA	Butterworth Legal Publishers, AUSTIN, Texas; BOSTON, Massachusetts; CLEARWATER, Florida (D & S Publishers); ORFORD, New Hampshire (Equity Publishing); ST PAUL, Minnesota; and SEATTLE, Washington

A CIP Catalogue record for this book is available from the British Library.

Front cover picture reproduced by
kind permission of The J Allan Cash
Photolibrary.

ISBN 0 406 11400 5
Printed in Great Britain by
Dotesios Printers Ltd, Trowbridge, Wiltshire

Preface

In his introduction to Selden's Table Talk, Frederick Pollock described a short work, a quarter of a century old, as being 'of the awkward age at which most books, except such as make themselves in some way necessary, have lost the freshness of youth and are not yet ripe for antiquity'. The present work on Church law, now more than half a century old, has undoubtedly lost the freshness of youth. Whether it has proved itself in some way necessary, in the course of several editions, is not for its author to say; but he may claim that his publishers, at least, in bringing out a sixth, do not judge it ripe for antiquity.

What has been consigned to antiquity is much of Church law itself. The reader may care to glance back for a moment. The book made its first appearance, with the blessing of Lord Atkin, in 1932, after the Church Assembly (Powers) Act 1919, and the Parochial Church Councils (Powers) Measure 1921, had introduced democratic self-government into the Church of England. But it was early days. The canons were still the canons of 1603, with an occasional addition by Convocation. Parliament had exerted its control over forms of worship by turning down the 'Deposited Book'. Section 1 of the Act of Uniformity of 1551 continued to impose a duty on all members of the Church of England to attend church on Sundays and holy days. Actions were brought to assert their right to do so, and even to claim that the ecclesiastical courts retained jurisdiction over the laity in matters of morality. A sentence of excommunication was still possible in law. The complexities of tithe rentcharge remained to afflict the pockets of parson and people.

But in 1965 came three Prayer Book Measures, authorising the use of new forms of service, and leading later to the Alternative Service Book of 1980: at last the Church of England had been able to revise its liturgy. The patient effort to reform the canon law, going back to 1939, began to show results, with the appearance of a first instalment of twenty-eight new canons. The Ecclesiastical Jurisdiction Measure 1963 did away, in whole or in part, with forty-eight previous enactments, preserving the jurisdiction of the Judicial Committee of the Privy Council in faculty suits only; and set up a new court, the Court of Ecclesiastical Causes Reserved, to try cases against clergymen involving doctrine, ritual or ceremonial. It abolished the jurisdiction to hear proceedings against lay officers.

Ten years after the Prayer Book Measures the changes had become so fundamental as almost to shake the foundations of ecclesiastical law. The General Synod of the Church of England had replaced the Assembly, and, for legislative purposes, the Convocations as well; and it is the Synod which makes the canons. Parliament, by giving its approval in 1974 to the Church of England (Worship and Doctrine) Measure, had yielded to the Synod control over forms of worship. The Pastoral Measure had provided for the reorganisation of the parishes, and for team ministries, manned by a new kind of rector and vicar, who had never known tithes, while the perpetual curate went at last to his rest. The repeal of section 1 of the Act of Uniformity, as 'no longer of practical utility', had gone without remark.

Today the change especially to be noticed is that in the status of women in the Church. The Sex (Disqualification) Removal Act was contemporary with the Church of England Assembly (Powers) Act, but its general impact

was strangely slow; and in Halsbury's Statutes, until after
the Second World War, the Act was classified under
Juries. In the first four editions of this work not much
more could be said than that a woman might be a churchwarden or a sexton, and might, at a pinch, baptise. But
in 1972 the Deaconesses and Lay Ministry Measure, fol-
lowed by Canon D 1, legislated for the order of deaconesses, enabling them to fill a comprehensive role in the
performance of the Church services. Then—one must not
say lastly—came in 1986 the Deacons (Ordination of
Women) Measure, and a woman may be ordained deacon.
As a result, deaconesses are a dwindling band: most of
those serving have been ordained, and are members of
the clergy of the Church of England.

In the work of recording this, and other significant
changes in Church law, the author has received outstanding help from the Rev. Canon John Dale, Vicar of
Hallow, Worcestershire, a solicitor and Registrar of the
Diocese of Worcester, who generously read the whole of
the manuscript, and made numerous suggestions for its
improvement. The Rev. F G Denman, Vicar of Sparkwell,
Devonshire, kindly indicated ways in which the subject
of parsonage houses might be more usefully treated. Mr
Brian J T Hanson, Legal Adviser to the General Synod,
has, as before, helped much with his advice, and with the
supply of material. It is a pleasure to the author—after
complaints made in previous editions—to acknowledge
the receipt of a complete set of the new canons. Mr
Hanson and his officers are to be congratulated on achiev-
ing a most convenient method of publication in loose leaf
form, kept up to date. To all of these the author extends
his warm thanks, while entering the usual reservation that
to him alone must be attributed any errors or short-
comings.

Lastly, he wishes to express his gratitude to his

publishers, Butterworths, whose long-standing services to writers—and, one hopes, to readers—are exemplified in the publication of this new edition.

20 Old Buildings   W. L. D.
Lincoln's Inn
May 1989

Contents

List of Cases

Table of Statutes and Measures

References in this table to *Statutes* are to Halsbury's Statutes of England (Fourth Edition) showing the volume and page at which the annotated text of the Act or Measure may be found. Page references printed in **bold** type indicate where the Act or Measure is set out in part or in full.

Table of Canons

References

Black Com	Blackstone's Commentaries, 5th ed., 1773.
Blew	Blew's *Organs and Organists*, 1878
Burn	Burn's *Ecclesiastical Law*, 9th edn, 1842.
Cripps	Cripps' *Law relating to the Church and Clergy*, 8th edn, 1937.
Degge	Degge's *Parson's Counsellor*, 7th edn, 1820.
Halsbury	Halsbury's Laws of England, 4th edn.
Opinions	Opinions of the Legal Advisory Commission of the General Synod, 6th edn
Phillimore	Phillimore's *Ecclesiastical Law*, 2nd edn, 1895
Prideaux	Prideaux's *Churchwardens' Guide*, 16th edn, 1895

CHAPTER ONE

Introduction

The law relating to the Church of England, the ecclesiastical law, is part of the general law of England.[1] It is enforced by special courts, the ecclesiastical courts, though to some extent also by the ordinary courts of law.[2]

The ecclesiastical law is drawn from three sources: these are the common law, the canon law, and statute law. The common law is that part of the law which is based on the common custom of the country. The canon law consists, first, of that part of the law of the Church of Rome which had been adopted in this country before the year 1533, either expressly by canons of the Church in England or impliedly by common consent and custom; and, secondly, of the canons and constitutions passed by national or provincial synods of the Church in England before the year 1533. But the canon law remains valid only so far as not repugnant to the laws of the realm or derogatory from the royal prerogative. This was the effect of the Submission of the Clergy Act 1533.[3] The statute law is

1 *Mackonochie v Lord Penzance* (1881) 6 App Cas 424 at 446.
2 See an article by Lord DENNING 'The Meaning of "Ecclesiastical Law"' in the Law Quarterly Review (1944), Vol 60, p 235.
3 See *Middleton v Crofts* (1736) 2 Atk 650 at 669, 670; *R v Millis* (1844) 10 Cl & Fin 534, HL, pp 680–682; and 1 Black Com 82, 83. More recent pronouncements on this matter, though in somewhat differing terms, are to be found in *Rector and Churchwardens of Bishopwearmouth v Adey* [1958] 3 All ER 441 at 443, and *Re St Mary's, Westwell* [1968] 1 All ER 631 at 633.

that part of the law which is contained in Acts of Parliament, and in Measures of the National Assembly, now the General Synod, of the Church of England.[1]

The ecclesiastical law as thus described, unless some provision of it is clearly limited to members of the Church of England, binds everyone, whether clerical or lay, and whether a member of the Church of England or not. But in addition to this old ecclesiastical law, there are the Canons.

The two Convocations, assemblies of the clergy for each of the provinces of Canterbury and York, had power to make Canons which, on receiving the royal assent, bound the clergy of the province in spiritual matters. In 1603 one hundred and forty-one Canons were made by Convocation of the province of Canterbury, and subsequently adopted by the Convocation of York.[2] The Canons of 1603 have now been repealed,[3] and a new code of Canons has been made by the General Synod of the Church of England.[4]

The legal position of the Church of England is different from that of every other religious body in this country, in that 'the State has accepted the Church as the religious body in its opinion truly teaching the Christian faith, and given to it a certain legal position, and to its decrees, if rendered under certain legal conditions, certain civil

1 There is also subordinate legislation (regulations, orders, schemes, and the like) under Acts and Measures.
2 As to the effect of the Canons, see *Case of Convocations* (1611) 12 Co Rep 72, *Middleton v Crofts* (1736) 2 Atk 650, and *Bishop of Exeter v Marshall* (1868) LR 3 HL 17.
3 Except for the proviso to Canon 113, which is reproduced on p 153 of the present code.
4 The Canons are published in loose leaf form, kept up to date, by Church House Publishing, Church House, Great Smith Street, London SW1P 3NZ.

sanctions'.[1] For this reason the Church of England is called the 'established' Church; and Canon A 1 refers to the 'Church of England, established according to the laws of this realm under the Queen's Majesty'. The 'legal position', given to the Church by the State, and denied to every other religious body, involves both privileges and disabilities. The following are the main features of the relationship between the State and the Church, in other words, of esablishment in England.[2]

(1) The Queen, just as she is head of the State, is also head of the Church. In the words of Canon A 7, the Queen, 'acting according to the laws of the realm, is the highest power under God in this kingdom, and has supreme authority over all persons in all causes, as well ecclesiastical as civil'. The sovereign must be in communion with the Church of England.[3] By virtue of her headship of the Church, the Queen is, for example, supreme Ordinary;[4] she directs the

1 PHILLIMORE J, in *Marshall v Graham* [1907] 2 KB 112 at 126.
2 This list does not pretend to be exhaustive. The reader may be referred to the Report of the Commission on Church and State (1952, CA 1023) for a further statement of the practical characteristics of establishment in England, and a discussion of the arguments for and against; and to 'Church and State' (1970, GS 19), being the Report of the Commission appointed in 1966 (the Chadwick Report), particularly Chapters 1 to 3. Further Reports of interest are those on 'Crown Appointments and the Church' (1964 CA 1543) and 'Synodical Government in the Church of England' (1966, CA 1600).
3 See the Bill of Rights 1688, and the Act of Settlement 1700, s 3.
It has long been the practice to display the royal arms in some churches to signify the royal supremacy, and a faculty will be granted for this purpose (*Re West Tarring Parish Church and Re St Paul, Battersea* [1954] 2 All ER 591 and 595). If the intention is to incorporate the arms in a memorial or window, the permission of the Home Office must be obtained (Times, 11 January 1957).
4 An Ordinary is an authority having jurisdiction in his own right,

Archbishops to summon Convocation; and she nomi-
the bishops for election by the chapters.[1]

(2) The faith, forms of worship, and rites and ceremonies
of the Church of England are controlled by or under
legislation. By the Church of England (Worship and
Doctrine) Measure 1974 control over forms of service
has been passed to the General Synod, subject to
certain limitations.

(3) All persons possess in general the right of baptism,
marriage, and burial according to the rites and ceremonies of the Church of England.[2]

(4) Every person who is not a member of a religious
body dissenting from the worship of the Church of
England has a right by law to attend divine service at
the parish church.

(5) The bishops and clergy have certain rights, and are
subject to certain disabilities, of a temporal nature.
For example, the senior bishops have seats in the
House of Lords;[3] on the other hand, the clergy of the
Church of England are not entitled to sit in the House
of Commons.[4]

---

and not as another's deputy. The archbishop is the Ordinary in his
province, and the bishop in his diocese. The judge of the bishop's
court, the chancellor, is also often referred to as the Ordinary. In
Basham v Lumley (1829) 3 C & P 489, it was held that the Governor
of a colony (in this case Bermuda) probably had the power of an
Ordinary.

1 For the preliminaries, see the Vacancy in See Committees Regulation
   1977 (an Act of Synod).
2 But see chapter 6 for qualifications of this principle.
3 The bishops entitled to sit in the House of Lords are the two
   Archbishops, the Bishops of London, Durham and Winchester, and
   twenty-one other bishops in order of seniority.
4 House of Commons (Clergy Disqualification) Act 1801, s 1. This
   disability extends to priests of the Roman Catholic Church (Roman
   Catholic Relief Act 1829, s 9). See also *Re MacManaway* [1951] AC
   161, which settled that clergy of the Church of Ireland also come

(6) The Church of England has, through the procedure provided by the Church of England Assembly (Powers) Act 1919 and the Synodical Government Measure 1969, a ready means of passing, by Measure, legislation having the effect of an Act of Parliament.

(7) The Church of England has its own courts, as already stated, in which is administered ecclesiastical law, and the decreees of these courts will be enforced by the State. On the other hand, the State courts will prohibit the ecclesiastical courts from exceeding their jurisdiction.[1]

The Church of England possesses a system of representative government, to be described in the next chapter, having some deep roots in the parishes. One of the first Measures to be passed by the Church Assembly under the enabling Act of 1919 was the Parochial Church Councils (Powers) Measure 1921 (later repealed and replaced by the Parochial Church Councils (Powers) Measure 1956[2]) which, by conferring powers on the newly constituted parochial church councils, effected a fundamental alteration in the government of the financial affairs of the parishes. The effect of the Measure was, broadly, to place control over matters affecting the finance of the parish church in the hands of the parochial church council; and the council, in this respect, fulfils the old functions

---

within the prohibition (ministers of the Church of Scotland are expressly prohibited by the Act of 1801); and see the Report of the Select Committee on Clergy Disqualification (H of C Paper 200 of 1953). The Chadwick Report (p 3, note 2, above) recommended alterations (para 187).

1 *R v St Edmundsbury and Ipswich Diocese, Chancellor, Ex p White* [1948] 1 KB 195; Ecclesiastical Jurisdiction Measure 1963, s 83 (2).
   On establishment as a whole, contrast the position of the Church in Wales under the Welsh Church Act 1914, which disestablished it.

2 Printed, as amended, in the Appendix, p 215, below.

of the vestry and the churchwardens. In respect of matters not directly involving the collection and expenditure of money on the fabric and services of the church, the former rights and duties of the churchwardens remain, for the most part, unaltered. They are still the officers of the Ordinary; they remain responsible for the order and discipline of the church and parish, and guardians of the rights of the parishioners in their church and churchyard; and the goods and ornaments of the church are vested in them.

These matters will be dealt with in detail in later chapters.

CHAPTER TWO

The Institutions of Church Government

The Synodical Government Measure 1969 established the General Synod of the Church of England as the principal governing body of the Church, replacing the National Assembly of the Church of England; and it transferred to the new body the powers of the Convocations of Canterbury and York to legislate by Canon. The Measure further constituted diocesan synods for the dioceses, and deanery synods for the deaneries, in place of the former diocesan and ruridecanal conferences; reformulated the statement of the general functions of parochial church councils contained in the Parochial Church Councils (Powers) Measure 1956; and revised the rules regulating the Representation of the Laity.

I. THE GENERAL SYNOD OF THE CHURCH OF ENGLAND

The General Synod consists of three Houses: the House of Bishops, formed by the Upper House of the Convocations joined together; the House of Clergy, formed by the Lower Houses of the Convocations joined together; and the House of Laity, elected in accordance with Part V of the Church Representation Rules contained in Schedule 3 to the Synodical Government Measure 1969.[1] The Con-

---

1 The Church Representation Rules as amended are set out in the Appendix to this work, beginning on p 134, below.

stitution of the General Synod is set out in Schedule 2 to the Measure.[1] It is the old Church Assembly renamed and reconstituted, and exercises the powers formerly possessed by the Assembly, with additions; and the most important of these additions is the power to make Canons. The Measure also transferred to the General Synod certain functions of the Convocations and the House of Laity of the Assembly.[2]

The main functions of the General Synod are, accordingly, to legislate on matters concerning the Church of England by Measure intended to be given the force and effect of an Act of Parliament, or by Canon. It may also consider, and express an opinion on, any matter of religious or public interest.[3] A motion for the final approval of a Measure or Canon must receive the assent of a majority of the members of each House present and voting, the Houses dividing separately unless the chairman and the Synod dispense with this requirement. In the case of motions on other matters a majority of all the members present and voting suffices, unless 25 of them demand a division by Houses.[4]

1　Several amendments have been made since. The Diocese in Europe Measure 1980 provides for the representation of the new diocese of Gibraltar in Europe in the Synod and Convocation of Canterbury.

2　Synodical Government Measure 1969, s 3.

3　Measure of 1969, Sch 2, para 6. The Synod may make orders or regulations or other subordinate instruments as authorised by Measure or Canon. It may proceed by Act of Synod or other instrument as appropriate when provision by or under a Measure or Canon is not required (eg Act of Synod of 10 November 1972 affirming and proclaiming the Central Stipends Authority Regulation (GS 109)).

4　Ibid, Sch 2, para 5. Special majorities are provided for in certain cases: see paras 5 (3) and 7 (5) of Sch 2, the Synodical Government (Special Majorities) Measure 1971, and s 1 of the Church of England (Miscellaneous Provisions) Measure 1978. See also chapter 6, p 48, below.

Any proposed provision touching doctrinal formulae or the services or ceremonies of the Church of England or the administration of the sacraments or sacred rites must be referred to the House of Bishops, for that House to agree the terms of the provision, before being submitted to the Synod for final approval. Further, the Convocations, or either of them, or the House of Laity, may require any such provision to be referred to them, in which case it must not be submitted to the Synod for final approval unless it has been approved by each House of the two Convocations sitting separately for their provinces, and by the House of Laity.[1]

A Measure providing for permanent changes in the services of baptism or holy communion or in the ordinal (the form of service used at ordinations), or any scheme for a constitutional union or a permanent and substantial change of relationship between the Church of England and another Christian body, a substantial number of whose members reside in Great Britain, is not to be finally approved by the Synod unless the Measure or scheme, or substance of it, has been approved by a majority of the diocesan synods.[2]

For the purpose of giving legislative force to Measures the General Synod elects a Legislative Committee, from members of all three Houses, to which Measures are referred when passed by the Synod. The Legislative Committee submits the Measure to the Ecclesiastical Committee of both Houses of Parliament, established under the Church of England Assembly (Powers) Act 1919. The Ecclesiastical Committee reports on the Measure to Parliament, and the report (which is published) and the text of the Measure are then laid before Parliament. If

1 Measure of 1969, Sch 2, para 7.
2 Ibid, Sch 2, para 8, amended by the Measure of 1971, and by the Synodical Government (Amendment) Measure 1974.

each House of Parliament passes a resolution that the Measure shall be presented to Her Majesty it is so presented, and on receiving the Royal Assent the Measure has the force and effect of an Act of Parliament.

The Church of England Assembly (Powers) Act 1919, and other enactments relating to the Church Assembly, were not repealed by the Measure of 1969. On the contrary, the Assembly having been 'renamed and reconstituted' by the Measure, references in the Act of 1919, and in all Measures, enactments and other instruments, to the Church Assembly, and its Constitution and to the Legislative Committee, are to be read as references, respectively, to the General Synod, and to its Constitution and to the Legislative Committee appointed thereunder.[1]

The general power to legislate by Canon, now vested in the General Synod instead of the Convocations, remains essentially a power to make rules for the clergy, and in spiritual matters only,[2] unless the power has been extended by statute in a particular context: examples of this are sections 4 (6) and 5 (5) of the 1969 Measure, relating to diocesan and deanery Synods; and, more

1   Measure of 1969, ss 1 and 2.
2   'And this notwithstanding that the laity now possess a third share in the process of making Canons, and notwithstanding the reasoning in para 32 of Appendix A to the Chadwick Report (see note 2 on p 3, above). In the first example given by the latter, the duty of the parties to a marriage service to accept the final decision of the minister regarding the music in accordance with Canon B 20, that Canon merely reflects—as does so much in the Canons—what is law *aliunde*: in this instance the common law right of the minister to control the manner of divine service (see p 80, below). As for the other example, the position of deaconesses and lay readers now (though not at the time of the Report) depends on the authorising Measure of 1972 (see p 29, below). This is not to deny that the laity may voluntarily put themselves in a position of obedience to the terms of a law which does not bind them directly; but that is a truism about every law, including a Canon.

important, the Church of England (Worship and Doctrine) Measure 1974.[1] The transfer of powers away from the Convocations included 'other functions of the [Convocations], and the authority, rights and privileges of the said [Convocations]'.[2] The provisions of sections 1 and 3 of the Submission of the Clergy Act 1533, requiring the Queen's assent and licence to the making, promulging and executing of Canons, and providing that no Canons shall be made or put in execution which are contrary or repugnant to the Royal prerogative or the customs, laws or statutes of the realm, were expressly applied by the Measure of 1969 to the Canons of the General Synod. The functions of the General Synod are of course exercisable for the Church of England as a whole, and not provincially.[3]

The General Synod comes into being, and is dissolved, automatically with the calling together of the Convocations, or their dissolution, as the case may be. It is to meet at least twice a year; and it has the two Archibishops as joint Presidents.[4]

2. THE CONVOCATIONS

The Convocations of Canterbury and York, and their ancient power to make Canons, have been mentioned in chapter 1. Convocation consists ordinarily of two Houses: the Upper House, containing the bishops of the province, and the Lower House, which includes representatives of the deans and provosts of cathedrals, an archdeacon from

1 See p 46, below.
2 Ibid, s 1 (1) and Sch 1, para 1. The wide language of the scheduled Canon is somewhat misleading. The Convocations did in fact retain a number of functions: see the next section of this chapter.
3 Measure of 1969, s 1.
4 Ibid, s 1 (4) and Sch 2, paras 3 and 4.

each diocese, proctors representing the parochial clergy, and a representative of the religious communities in the province.[1] The power to make Canons was transferred to the General Synod, by Canon in the form set out in Schedule 1 to the Synodical Government Measure 1969. The Convocations continue to meet separately for the purpose of considering matters concerning the Church of England, and of making such provision for them as is appropriate otherwise than by Canon, or referring them to the General Synod, and in respect of other matters.[2] Their powers under Article 7 of the Constitution of the General Synod in relation to proposed legislation touching doctrinal formulae and like matters have already been mentioned.[3]

Convocations may provide for joining to their two Houses, at such sittings and for such purposes as it determines, a House of Laity, composed of the members of the House of Laity of the General Synod elected for, and other representatives from, the province.[4]

3. THE DIOCESAN SYNODS

Section 4 of the Synodical Government Measure 1969 required that diocesan synods be constituted for the dioceses. Their functions are (a) to consider and make provision for matters concerning the Church of England in relation to the diocese, and to consider and express their

1 Canon H 2. The Synodical Government (Amendment) Measure 1974 authorises provision by Canon to enable some of the suffragan bishops to sit in the Upper House.
2 See the Church of England (Worship and Doctrine) Measure 1974 (chapter 6, p 46, below) and the Ecclesiastical Jurisdiction Measure 1963, ss 9, and 35–37.
3 See p 9, above.
4 Measure of 1969, Sch 1, para 3.

opinion on any other matters of religious or public interest (but they may not issue statements purporting to declare the doctrine of the Church); (b) to advise the bishop on any matters on which he may consult the synod (and it is his duty to consult it on matters of general concern and importance to the diocese); and (c) to consider and express their opinion on any matters referred to them by the General Synod, and in particular to approve or disapprove provisions referred to them by the General Synod under Article 8 of the Constitution.[1] The diocesan synods are required to keep the deanery synods informed of the policies and problems of the diocese and of the business which is to come before meetings of the diocesan synods, and may delegate executive functions to deanery synods. Moreover, they are also to keep themselves informed, through the deanery synods, of events and opinion in the parishes, and to give opportunities for discussing at meetings of the diocesan synod matters raised by deanery synods and parochial church councils. All functions that were exercisable by the diocesan conferences were transferred to the diocesan synods.

Part IV of the Church Representation Rules provides for the constitution and membership of diocesan synods. They consist of the bishop, a house of clergy and a house of laity. The two houses (approximately equal in numbers) are elected every three years by the house of clergy or house of laity, as the case may be, of the deanery synod. They also contain ex-officio and co-opted members.[2]

1 See p 9, above.
2 The bishop may nominate up to ten additional members, clergy or laity; Rule 24 (4).

   If a diocese is divided into episcopal areas under the Dioceses Measure 1978, area synods may be constituted, in which case the Church Representation Rules apply as if the area synods were diocesan synods (s 17).

4. THE DEANERY SYNODS

Under s 5 of the Synodical Government Measure deanery synods took over from the ruri-decanal conferences. Their functions are (a) the same, for the deanery, as the first of the functions of the diocesan synods for the diocese;[1] (b) to bring together the views of the parishes of the deanery on common problems, to discuss and formulate common policies on these problems, to foster a sense of community and interdependence among those parishes, and generally to promote in the deanery the whole mission of the Church, pastoral, evangelistic, social and ecumenical; (c) to make known and so far as appropriate put into effect any provision made by the diocesan synod; (d) to consider the business of the diocesan synod, and particularly any matters referred to that synod by the General Synod, and to sound parochial opinion whenever they are required or consider it appropriate to do so; and (e) to raise with the diocesan synod such matters as the deanery synod considers appropriate. If the diocesan synod delegates to deanery synods functions in relation to the parishes of their deaneries, and in particular the determination of parochial shares in quotas of expenditure allocated to the deaneries, the deanery synods are to exercise these functions.

Under Part III of the Church Representation Rules the deanery synods are to consist of a house of clergy and a house of laity. The former is composed of the clerks in holy orders beneficed in or licensed to any parish in the deanery, and certain other clergymen licensed or resident in the deanery. The house of laity consists of the parochial representatives elected every three years to the synod by the annual meetings of the parishes in the deanery, lay members of the General Synod or diocesan synod whose

1 See p 12, above, under (a).

names are on the roll of a parish in the deanery, and other lay members, being deaconesses or whole-time licensed lay workers, as determined by the diocesan synod. Additional members may be co-opted by either house. The house of laity is not to be less in number than the house of clergy.[1]

5. THE PAROCHIAL CHURCH COUNCILS

The parishes form the basis of the structure of Church government. The parochial church councils are elected by the members of the Church of England resident or worshipping in the parish, at the annual parochial church meeting, and these same persons elect the parochial representatives in the houses of laity in the deanery synods, which houses in turn elect the members of the houses of laity of the diocesan synods.[2] The House of Laity of the General Synod also is elected by the members of the houses of laity of the deanery synod. The provisions of the Synodical Government Measure under which the parishes can make their views known in the deanery and diocesan synods have just been mentioned.

The constitution and functions of the parochial church councils will be discussed in detail in the ensuing part of this work.[3] Their particular functions were in the main left untouched by the legislation of 1969, but the statement of their general functions was broadened. The primary duty now of the minister and the council is to *consult together* on matters of general concern and importance to

1 Rule 22 of the Church Representation Rules empowers a diocesan synod to provide by scheme for the representation of cathedral clergy and lay persons on a deanery synod.
2 See chapter 4 and the Church Representation Rules in the Appendix for the details.
3 See especially chapters 4 and 8.

the parish. There is early recognition in the section of the purpose of promoting the whole mission of the Church in the parish, a task falling primarily on the incumbent as the spiritual leader, but in the accomplishment of which he may look to the co-operation of the council as its foremost function.[1]

1 See s 6 of the Synodical Government Measure 1969, replacing s 2 of the Parochial Church Councils (Powers) Measure 1956 (Appendix 3, below, p 215).

As to co-operation, see *Re St Peter, Roydon*, [1969] 2 All ER 1233.

CHAPTER THREE

The Incumbent

I. THE BENEFICE

It will not be amiss to begin this chapter with a paragraph
or two on terminology. The 'incumbent' is, strictly, the
clergyman in possession of the benefice, or living; he may
be rector or vicar;[1] and he has, under the bishop, the
exclusive cure of souls in the benefice. From this conception flow the legal rules defining the duties, and the
rights, of the incumbent set forth in this and the succeeding chapters. But some inroads into principle have
been made by the legislation providing in recent years for
the reorganisation of the parishes. In a benefice where
there is a team ministry[2] there is both rector and vicar, or
vicars: the rector is the incumbent, but a vicar is given 'a
status equal to that of an incumbent of a benefice'; and to
a vicar there may be assigned 'a special cure of souls' in
a part of it, and the name of vicar of a church in that

1 Perpetual curacies were turned into vicarages by s 8 of the Pastoral
  Measure 1968.
  Originally the rector (or parson) had full rights to all the ecclesiastical dues, especially the tithes, in the parish. If the living had been
  appropriated he was the vicar, often with a share only of the tithes.
  A perpetual curate had no tithes at all. For a long time little practical
  significance had attached to this difference between a rector and a
  vicar, and the terms were given a new connotation by the Pastoral
  Measure 1968.
2 See p 20, below.

part.[1] A Measure may contain an extended definition of 'incumbent' for its own purposes. For example, for the important purpose of the decisions regarding forms of service to be taken jointly by the incumbent and the parochial church council under the Church of England (Worship and Doctrine) Measure 1974,[2] 'incumbent' includes a curate licensed to the charge of the parish, a minister acting as priest-in-charge of the parish where the rights of presentation have been suspended, and a vicar in a team ministry assigned a special cure of souls; and the Ecclesiastical Jurisdiction Measures apply to vicars in a team ministry as if they were incumbents of the benefice.[3]

The term 'minister' may be used, especially where the emphasis is ecclesiastical, or at any rate liturgical. It is the word used in the rubrics to the Book of Common Prayer itself, in the Alternative Service Book, and in the Canons. It has a wider meaning than 'incumbent', and often simply means the officiating clergyman. It is the term used in sections 7 and 8 of the Parochial Church Councils (Powers) Measure 1956, the Church Representation Rules,[4] and the Parochial Registers and Records Measure 1978.[5] But 'incumbent' is used in section 2 of the Powers Measure,[6] which section lays down the fundamental functions respectively of the incumbent and council.

While therefore the primary conception of 'incumbent' remains, the legislature has considerably extended the ambit of the term. It would not make sense to contend

1 Pastoral Measure 1983, s 20.
2 See p 47, below.
3 Pastoral Measure 1983, s 20 (9).
4 Where it is given a similar meaning (rule 44) to 'incumbent' in the Worship and Doctrine Measure.
5 For varying definitions see s 2 (5), 3 (5) and 9 (8). 'Incumbent' is also used; and s 2 (3) refers to 'the incumbent or priest in charge'.
6 As substituted by s 6 of the Synodical Government Measure 1969.

that, for example, a priest-in-charge of a parish during the suspension of presentation rights is not an 'incumbent' for the seminal purposes of section 2 of the Parochial Church Councils (Powers) Measure 1956; and his parishioners may naturally and legitimately think of him as such, especially if he is living in the parsonage house.

'Benefice' is defined in the Interpretation Measure 1925 to include an endowed public chapel, a private chapelry, and a chapelry or district belonging or annexed to any church or chapel. But it does not usually include the office of vicar in a team ministry, for example for the purposes of the Patronage (Benefices) Measure 1986, the Pastoral Measure 1983 (but see section 85), the Endowments and Glebe Measure 1976, and the Repair of Benefice Buildings Measure 1972. It does, however, include the office of vicar in a team ministry for the purposes of the Incumbents (Vacation of Benefices) Measure 1977.

A 'parish' for ecclesiastical purposes is ordinarily a district committed to the charge of one incumbent: a conventional district is not a 'parish' (unless treated as such for a special purpose, as in the Church Representation Rules), and remains within the mother parish.[1] The Pastoral Measure 1968 converted all existing districts constituted for ecclesiastical purposes, except conventional districts, into parishes, and the minister into a vicar.[2]

We can now consider the Pastoral Measure 1983. It begins by requiring the appointment for every diocese of a pastoral committee, to which is given the duty of reviewing from time to time the arrangements for pastoral supervision in the diocese, and, if it considers it desirable,

---

1 Black Com 111; Pastoral Measure 1983, s 86 (1); Church Representation Rules, rule 44; and see p 114, below.
2 See p 114, below for a fuller statement.

making recommendations to the bishop which will lead to a pastoral scheme or order.[1] A scheme may provide for the creation (by union or otherwise) of new benefices[2] or parishes, the dissolution or alteration of the areas of benefices or parishes, the creation of extra-parochial places or their incorporation in parishes, the making of sharing agreements in respect of a church or parsonage house,[3] the holding of benefices in plurality, and the establishment of 'team ministries' and 'group ministries'. A team ministry is to share the cure of souls within the area of a benefice, which, if it is not already a rectory, is to be a rectory, and the incumbent a rector; his office will either be freehold or for a term of years, and he will be a corporation sole, and hold the property of the benefice. The other ministers in the team will be vicars, with a 'status equal to that of an incumbent of a benefice';[4] and pastoral care will be shared with such other persons as are authorised by the bishop to serve as members of the team.[5] The rector, leading the team, has the general responsibility for the cure of souls within the benefice. A vicar in a team ministry has, for his term of years, the same security of tenure, and in general the same authority to perform the offices and services, as an incumbent of a benefice. The bishop may, however, assign to a vicar a social cure of souls for an area within the benefice, or a special responsibility for a particular pastoral function,

1 A scheme is made by the Church Commissioners, an order by the bishop.
2 Which will be vicarages unless resulting from a union or dissolution involving a rectory, or a team ministry is established (s 23).
3 See the Sharing of Church Buildings Act 1969.
4 The Ecclesiastical Jurisdiction Measures 1963 and 1974 apply to vicars in a team ministry as if they were incumbents of the benefice; and in the Incumbents (Vacation of Benefices) Measure 1977, 'benefice' includes the office of such a vicar (s 19). And see p 19, above.
5 Pastoral Measure 1983, s 20 (1) (b).

and independent of the rector's general responsibility; or he may assign to a vicar a general responsibility to be shared with the rector for the cure of souls in the whole benefice. The team is to meet at regular intervals to discuss and reach a common mind on matters of general concern or special interest to the team ministry.

If a 'group ministry' is established for a group of benefices, the incumbent of any benefice in the group may perform the offices and services in the other benefices within the group, but in accordance with any directions of the incumbent of the other benefice. The incumbents are to assist each other so as to make the best possible provision for the cure of souls throughout the area of the group ministry, and meet as a chapter as provided for a team ministry.

There are provisions for the designation of parish churches; and for the licensing by the bishop, where a parish has no church, of buildings to be used as places of worship, and of a 'parish centre of worship', which will then be deemed to be the parish church for nearly all purposes.[1] There are also provisions relating to redundant churches, to churchyards and burial grounds, parsonage houses, endowments and stipends, and to patronage; the patron of a new benefice will be the diocesan board of patronage unless a scheme provides otherwise.[2]

A pastoral committee, before making its rec-ommendations to the bishop, must so far as practicable

---

1 Pastoral Measure 1983, ss 27 and 29. See further pp 53, 61, below, as to the rights of parishioners where there is more than one parish church.

2 Ibid, ss 28 and 30 to 33. See further as to patronage p 23, below.

  Part III of the Pastoral Measure contains elaborate provisions to deal with the problem of redundant churches. It sets up statutory bodies, makes further provision in relation to pastoral schemes, authorising redundancy schemes, and provides for many incidental matters.

ascertain the views of 'interested parties', including incumbents, patrons and parochial church councils (or, if there is no council, the churchwardens).[1] The bishop submits proposals to the Church Commissioners who again give interested parties an opportunity to comment, and the scheme, if the Commissioners decide to make it, is subject to confirmation by Order in Council.[2] If the proposals fall within the classes of case specified in section 37 of the Measure that can be dealt with by order, and if the Commissioners approve them, an order will be made by the bishop, and not a scheme.

2. APPOINTMENT OF INCUMBENT

Only a priest may be admitted to a benefice (Canon C 10), and the bishop may refuse to institute anyone with less than three years experience as a full-time parochial minister (Benefices Measure 1972). The Ecclesiastical Offices (Age Limit) Measure 1975 has subjected an incumbent—together with an archbishop, a bishop, and other Church dignitaries—to an age limit. A clergyman who has reached the age of seventy may not be presented to a benefice, or appointed vicar in a team ministry. An incumbent or vicar in a team ministry must, on reaching seventy, vacate his office unless he has held it since before 1 August 1975; but if the bishop considers that the pastoral needs of the parish or diocese make it desirable, he may with the consent of the parochial church council authorise extension up to two years. An incumbent vacates his living by signing an instrument of resignation.

1 Ss 3, 84.
2 Ss 4 to 9. Provision is made for appeal, with leave, to the Judicial Committee of the Privy Council, against a scheme. It is a 'genuine appeal process ... not to be compared with judicial review' (*Hargreaves v Church Commissioners* [1983] 3 All ER 17).

The right of presentation to a living—the advowson—is held by the patron. The right has been much restricted in recent years, and the law is now contained in the Patronage (Benefices) Measure 1986. The Measure is long and detailed, and what follows is but a summary of its more important provisions.

The registrar of the diocese maintains a register of patrons, and the patron must register before he can exercise any of his functions. A right of patronage cannot be sold. It may, however, be transferred by gift or will, or by pastoral scheme or order; but if by gift (or exchange) only on the conditions contained in section 3 of the Measure and Schedule 1. The parochial church council may make representations; and, if it is the diocesan board of patronage wishing to transfer a right of patronage, the council's consent must be obtained.

The exercise of the right of presentation is regulated by Part II. If the patron is an individual and not a clergyman, he must make a declaration that he is an actual communicant member of the Church of England[1] or of a Church in communion with it; otherwise he must appoint a representative. The parochial church council is to meet within four weeks of the sending by the diocesan authority of notice of a vacancy, and then proceed as required by sections 11 and 12 of the Measure. The chief purposes of the meeting will be to prepare a statement, to be sent to the patron and the bishop, describing the conditions, needs and traditions of the parish, to appoint two lay members as the council's representatives in connection with the selection of an incumbent, to decide whether to request the patron to consider advertising the vacancy, and to decide whether to request a meeting with the bishop and the patron. If the council does not appoint

1 See the definition on p 35, note 2, below.

two representatives, the churchwardens will act as representatives.[1]

No offer of the living may be made until the offer is approved (or deemed to be approved as laid down) both by the bishop and the representatives of the parish. If approval is not forthcoming, the patron may ask for a review by the archbishop; and the archbishop may authorise the presentation.[2] Various ancillary rights attaching to patronage have been abolished.[3]

Section 67 of the Pastoral Measure 1983 enables the bishop, with the consent of the pastoral committee and after consulting the patron and the parochial church council,[4] by notice given within three months before a benefice is to become vacant or at any time during vacancy, to require that the right of presentation shall not be exercised, for a period not exceeding five years, without the consent of the pastoral committee and the bishop. The bishop may continue the suspension for successive periods of five years. The churchwardens, who will receive a copy of the notice, must affix it at or near the church door. The bishop appoints sequestrators for the currency of the suspension, who will, in accordance with

---

1   The provisions of ss 11 and 12 of the Measure are very detailed, and are set out in the Appendix, p 231, below. The Patronage (Benefices) Rules 1987 (SI 1987/773) contain rules concerning the registration and transfer of rights of patronage, and the exercise of rights of presentation, and forms.

2   The duty of the archbishop is to consider the interests of the benefice, and he is not required to hold a quasi-judicial inquiry (*R v Archbishop of Canterbury* [1944] 1 All ER 179).

3   See s 34. Special provisions apply to advowsons held by trustees for sale or comprised in settled land (s 33), and to benefices in the patronage of the Crown or the Lord Chancellor (ss 35 and 36).

4   As to what is sufficient 'consultation', see *Re Union of Benefices of Whippingham and East Cowes, St James, Derham v Church Comrs for England* [1954] AC 245.

any directions the bishop may give after consulting the parochial church council, and the patron so far as reasonably practicable, make provision for the performance of the ecclesiastical duties of the benefice.[1]

After presentation, admission to the cure of souls is by means of institution by the bishop; and the minister is put into complete possession of the benefice and its emoluments, and the parsonage house and any glebe land vested in the diocesan board of finance under section 15 of the Endowments and Glebe Measure, by means of induction, usually by the archdeacon.[2]

3. RESIDENCE

The incumbent is required to reside on his benefice. The Pluralities Act 1838 still governs this subject, s 32 providing that 'every spiritual person holding any benefice shall keep residence on his benefice, and in the house of residence (if any) belonging thereto'. The penalty for not doing so is, if the absence is for more than three months in a year but not more than six months, forfeiture of a third of the annual value of the benefice. For longer absences the forfeiture is correspondingly increased.[3] If

1 Pastoral Measure 1983, s 68, and Sch 7. Section 69 of the Measure imposes restrictions on presentation pending the making of pastoral schemes or orders.

2 Induction may be by proxy (Phillimore, p 355). If the bishop is the patron, he 'collates' to the living. When there are two or more parish churches, or benefices are held in plurality, induction to one suffices, as directed by the bishop (Pastoral Measure 1983, s 75). Modifications of the requirements in relation to admission and induction, when there has been a pastoral scheme or order, are contained in para 5 of Sch 3 to the Pastoral Measure 1983.

3 The penalties are sued for in the consistory court by a person authorised by the bishop. Benefices are not to be held in plurality except under a pastoral scheme or order (Pastoral Measure 1983, ss 18 and 85).

there is no house, or no fit house, of residence, the bishop
may license the incumbent to reside in 'some fit and
convenient house' not belonging to the benefice, so long
as it is within three miles of the parish church (or two
miles in a town). Houses bought or built by the Church
Commissioners as residences, not in the parish but conveniently near thereto, are, if approved by the bishop, the
proper houses of residence.[1]

The bishop may grant a licence dispensing with residence altogether on certain specified grounds, eg incapacity, or the dangerous illness of the incumbent's wife
or child. In cases not specified the archbishop must
approve the licence. All licences for non-residence expire
on 31 December in the year following the year in which
they are granted. Where an incumbent is not residing on
his benefice, the bishop may appoint a curate to perform
his duties.[2]

To an incumbent who fails to reside on his benefice the
bishop may, instead of or after proceeding against him for
the penalties mentioned above, issue a monition requiring
him to reside. If the monition is disobeyed the profits of

1 See also Canon C 25; s 31 of the Pastoral Measure 1983 as to places
of residence for incumbents and vicars in team ministries in respect
of benefices created or affected by pastoral schemes; and s 68 (3) as to
the residence in the parsonage house of a curate-in-charge appointed
during a suspension period. Where a scheme provides for union of
two benefices, it may provide for the incumbent to reside in the
smaller parish (*Hargreaves v Church Commissioners* [1983] 3 All ER
17). Under s 24 of the Endowments and Glebe Measure 1976 a vicar
in a team ministry may be permitted to reside rent free in a house
on diocesan glebe land.

2 The widow of an incumbent may continue to live in the parsonage
for two months after her husband's death (Pluralities Act 1838,
s 36).

   See ss 71 (4) and 72 of the Ecclesiastical Jurisdiction Measure
1963 as to appointment of a curate, and his residence in the parsonage
house, during the suspension or inhibition of the incumbent.

the benefice may be sequestrated, and out of the proceeds of sequestration the stipend of any curate appointed to serve the benefice will be paid. If sequestration continues for a year, or there are two sequestrations within two years, the benefice becomes vacant.

Any agreement made for letting the parsonage house will be void if the bishop orders the incumbent to reside there (or assigns the house as a residence for a curate); and if the tenant remains in possession after being served with a copy of the bishop's order he is liable to a penalty.[1] The Rent Acts have never applied to parsonage houses.[2] The Rent Act 1968 authorises the recovery of possession of other dwellinghouses subject to a 'regulated tenancy' under the Act, if held for the purpose of occupation by a minister of religion.[3]

The Parsonages Measures 1938 and 1947, together with

1 Pluralities Act 1838, s 59.
2 *Bishop of Gloucester v Cunnington* [1943] KB 101. This is so even if the incumbent wishes to re-let it (*Brandon v Grundy* [1943] 2 All ER 208); and a cottage in the parsonage grounds, if 'necessary for the convenient occupation' of the parsonage, is also outside the Acts (*Culverwell v Larcombe* (1945) 61 TLR 385; *Neale v Jennings* [1946] KB 238). But a house left to a diocesan trust on terms which gave the trustees a discretion to allow use as a residence for the clergy or not, *is* within the Acts (*Worcester Diocesan Trust Registered v Taylor* (1947) 177 LT 581); and so is a house built, and required, as a residence for a mere assistant priest (*Jackson v Hill* (1948) 98 LJ 537—county court decision). See Megarry, *The Rent Acts* (11th edn p 138), for further details.

Under s 56 (1) of the Town and Country Planning Act 1971 an 'ecclesiastical building which is for the time being used for ecclesiastical purposes' is exempt from the control imposed by Part IV of the Act over a 'listed' building; and see *A-G v Howard United Reform Church Trustees, Bedford* [1976] AC 363 as the the meaning of the phrase. But a building 'used or availble for use by a minister of religion wholly or mainly as a residence from which he performs the duties of his office' is not within the exemption.
3 Sch 3, Part I, Case 11.

a number of older enactments,[1] contain rules governing the sale, purchase and improvement of parsonage houses. The Repair of Benefice Buildings Measure 1972 replaced the earlier Ecclesiastical Dilapidations Measures, putting the duty of keeping parsonage houses in repair on the diocesan parsonages boards created under the Measure; or if no board has been set up, on the diocesan board of finance. The duty extends to the structure and exterior of the buildings, the heating, water and sanitation installations, and fences, gates and drives; but not to glebe buildings.[2] The board will insure. The incumbent has the same duty to take care of his house as has an ordinary tenant, and he must notify the board of any repairs appearing necessary. He must not add to or alter the buildings without the consent of the board and the patron, and must keep the board informed of matters affecting the property such as Government and public authority notices.[3] The board has power to defray rates and other outgoings.[4]

The incumbent can apply to the local authority for a grant, under Part VII of the Housing Act 1974, towards the conversion of his house or buildings to provide increased housing accommodation, or towards the improvement or repair of the house.

---

1 The reader may be referred to Cripps, p 418. See also Part I of the Church Property (Miscellaneous Provisions) Measure 1960, and s 4 of the Church of England (Miscellaneous Provisions) Measure 1983, amending the Parsonages Measure of 1938. Any part of a parsonage house (or land) not required for the convenient occupation of the incumbent or as the residence house of a benefice may be transferred by the Church Commissioners to the diocesan board of finance (Endowments and Glebe Measure 1976, s 32).
2 S 2.
3 S 13.
4 Ss 21 and 23.

4. PERFORMANCE OF DUTIES

The duties which the incumbent is called upon to perform
are set out in the following chapters. The provision made
by the Pastoral Measure 1983 for team and group ministries has already been described.[1] The incumbent may
have the assistance of deacons, deaconesses, licensed lay
workers, readers and other lay persons in the performance
of the services. The Deaconesses and Lay Ministry
Measure 1972 enabled the General Synod to provide by
Canon for extending the ministry of these persons; and
under Canon D 1 a deaconess may be authorised to
say or sing morning or evening prayer (save for the
absolution), to distribute the sacrament and read the
epistle and gospel at holy communion, to preach, church
women and baptise, to perform the burial service with
the goodwill of the persons responsible, and to publish
banns of marriage. Canon E 4 prescribes the functions of
lay readers.[2]

A more fundamental change was introduced by the
Deacons (Ordination of Women) Measure 1986, enabling
provision by Canon for the ordination of women as
deacons (not priests). Canon 4A provides accordingly. In
any Canon, order, rule or regulation relating to deacons,
words imparting the masculine gender include the femi-
nine, unless the contrary intention appears.[3]

Two Measures are directed to securing the proper
performance of clerical duties. The first, and generally
more important, is the Incumbents (Vacation of Benefices)
Measure 1977, replacing the narrower Incumbents (Disability) Measure 1945. It provides for the institution of
an enquiry, in two types of situation, the first being 'a

1 P 20, above.
2 See also pp 51, 56, 66 below.
3 The Measure also makes provision for pension rights.

serious breakdown of the pastoral relationship between the incumbent and his parishioners to which the conduct of the incumbent or of his parishioners or of both has contributed over a substantial period' (Part I of the Measure). The enquiry may be requested by the incumbent, the archdeacon, or a two-thirds majority of lay members of the parochial church council (present and voting). The request is made in writing to the bishop and the secretary of the diocesan synod and must contain particulars of the facts thought to justify the enquiry. If made by the parochial church council, the request must be signed (with addresses) by all the persons making it, state that they constitute the majority required, specify two to act as representatives, and state which of these two (the 'designated representative') will conduct correspondence. Unless the request is made by the archdeacon, or he himself is the incumbent, the bishop will direct the archdeacon to take such steps as he considers appropriate to promote better relations between incumbent and parishioners, and remove the causes of their estrangement. If the archdeacon reports in favour of an enquiry, or it was he who requested one, or is the incumbent, the bishop will direct that an enquiry be held. He will further direct one if, though the archdeacon did not originally report in favour of one, within six months either the archdeacon, the incumbent, the secretary of the parochial church council or the designated representative informs the bishop that an enquiry is needed; except that, where the incumbent has held his office for less than three years, or it is the secretary of the council or the designated representative asking for an enquiry, the bishop has a discretion. An enquiry will be conducted by a diocesan committee unless the incumbent, within fourteen days of receiving notice of his right to make an election, opts for a provincial tribunal. The incumbent may at any time stop the proceedings by offering his resignation, so long as the bishop accepts it.

The second situation provided for by the Measure of 1977 is that which was covered by the Incumbents (Disability) Measure 1945. The bishop may institute a diocesan committee of enquiry to enquire whether an incumbent is 'unable by reason of age or infirmity of mind or body to discharge adequately the duties attaching to his benefice, and, if so, whether it is desirable that he should resign his benefice or be given assistance in discharging those duties.'

A diocesan committee will consist of three clergymen, and two lay persons, from panels chosen respectively by the house of clergy and house of laity of the diocesan synod.[1] A provincial tribunal will consist of five members appointed by the Vicar-General from outside the diocese: the chairman will be either the diocesan chancellor or a Queen's Counsel, the other members two clergymen and two lay persons, communicants. The incumbent may object to any member of a committee or tribunal. He may give evidence and call witnesses. He may be assisted, or in his absence represented, professionally or otherwise. The parochial church council may make representations in either case and, if the enquiry is before a tribunal, be legally represented. Also, *any* person may make written representations to a committee or tribunal.[2]

The committee or tribunal reports to the bishop whether in its opinion there has been a serious breakdown of the pastoral relationship, and, if so, whether the conduct of the incumbent or the parishioners or both has contributed to it over a substantial period; or it may report that the incumbent is unable by reason of age

1 See the Schedule to the Measure. Para 4 gives the procedure.
2 Para 12 of the Schedule.

or infirmity of mind or body to discharge his duties adequately. If the committee or tribunal reports affirmatively, it will make recommendations as to the action to be taken by the bishop. Various courses are open to him. In the case of breakdown the most serious is to declare the benefice vacant, provided at least four members of the committee or tribunal have so recommended; other courses are the imposition of disqualifications on the incumbent, a rebuke to him or the parishioners as may be appropriate, and pastoral advice and guidance. Other measures are available in a case of inability to discharge the duties (section 11). An incumbent whose benefice has been declared vacant or who has resigned must vacate the parsonage house within three months. Provision is made for compensation to the incumbent, payment of pension, and costs and expenses, in appropriate cases (sections 13–16).

The second Measure referred to above is the Ecclesiastical Jurisdiction Measure 1963, which enables proceedings to be taken against an incumbent for conduct unbecoming to the office and work of a clerk in holy orders, or for serious, persistent or continuous neglect of duty. As this involves the jurisdiction of the ecclesiastical courts the matter can most conveniently be dealt with in chapter thirteen.

CHAPTER FOUR

Parochial Organisation

I. THE CHURCH ELECTORAL ROLL

The parochial church council is responsible for compiling and keeping up to date a church electoral roll, and must appoint a church electoral roll officer for the purpose. The roll contains the names, and addresses where practicable, of lay members of the Church of England,[1] of either sex, who have reached the age of sixteen. To be on the roll a person must have been baptised, must either be resident in the parish or have habitually attended public worship there for six months before enrolment, and must sign the form, given in the Church Representation Rules, containing the declarations there set out.[2] If a person is qualified to be on the roll of more than one parish he is entitled to be on the roll of each parish. The roll must be revised annually after notice given to that effect; and the revised roll, with a list of any names removed, must be exhibited on or near the church door for at last fourteen days before the annual parochial church meeting. Reference should be made to rules 1, 2 and 3 of the Church Representation Rules for further details relating to the

1 And of any Church in communion with the Church of England.
2 Rule 1 of the Church Representation Rules (see Appendix, p 136). In this chapter 'rule' means one of these rules.

Before a council is constituted the minister and churchwardens will compile the roll.

formation and revision of the roll, and to rule 36 regarding appeals.[1] The number of names on the roll must be certified to the secretaries of the diocesan and deanery synods.[2] In 1990, and in every succeeding sixth year, a new roll is to be prepared; and everyone must apply for inclusion on it, whether or not on the existing roll.

2. THE PAROCHIAL CHURCH MEETING

All lay persons whose names are on the roll are entitled to attend the annual parochial church meeting. Clerks in holy orders, beneficed in or licensed to the parish or any other parish in the area of the benefice to which the parish belongs, or merely resident in the parish if not beneficed in or licensed to another parish, are entitled to attend; also, if the parish is in the area of a group ministry, incumbents of benefices in the group.[3] The meeting is to be held not later than 30 April in each year. The minister convenes the meeting and presides. He may also convene a special parochial church meeting; and he must do so if requested in writing by one-third of the lay members of the parochial church council.[4]

The annual meeting receives from the council, and is free to discuss, a copy of the electoral roll, its annual reports and audited accounts,[5] an audited statement of its funds and property, a report on the fabric, goods and

1 Note the case of *Stuart v Haughley Parochial Church Council* [1936] Ch 32, in which an injunction was granted by the high court requiring the restoration to the roll of names improperly removed by the council. Rule 1 (7) now specifies the grounds for removing a name.

2 Rule 4.

3 Rule 5.

4 Rules 6, 7 and 18. The archdeacon may be requested to convene an extraordinary parochial church meeting, or meeting of the parochial church council (Rule 18).

5 See p 88, below.

ornaments of the church, and a report on the proceedings
of the deanery synod. If the accounts and statement are
approved by the meeting, the chairman signs them and
gives them to the council for publication. The meeting
appoints auditors of the council; and anyone entitled to
attend may ask questions about parochial church matters,
or bring about a discussion of any matter of parochial or
general church interest, by moving a general resolution
or moving to give a particular recommendation to the
council in relation to its duties.[1]

Important business of the annual meeting is to elect
parochial representatives of the laity to the deanery synod
(every third year) and to the parochial church council,
and to elect sidesmen (to be done in that order). To be
elected a member of the deanery synod or the council
a person must be on the electoral roll, and an actual
communicant member of the Church of England, or, in
the case of election to the council, of any Church in
communion with the Church of England.[2] To be elected
to the deanery synod, a person must be eighteen, to the
council, seventeen. To be qualified to be elected a sidesman a person's name need merely be on the electoral roll.
Before being elected a person should give his consent, or
at least there should be sufficient evidence of his willingness to serve.[3] He may be an elected member of a body

1 Rule 8.
2 'Actual communicant member of the Church of England' is defined
  in rule 44 (1) as a member of the Church of England who is
  confirmed or ready and desirous of being confirmed and has received
  communion according to the use of the Church of England or of a
  Church in communion with the Church of England at least three
  times in the preceding twelve months. See also rule 9 (1A) as to the
  election of a person 'of communicant status in another Church
  which subscribes to the doctrine of the Holy Trinity'.
3 Rule 9.

though also an ex-officio member.[1] The meeting decides
the number of elected representatives to the council; and
they remain in office until the next annual meeting unless
it decides that a third of the members should retire each
year.[2] Where there is more than one place of worship in
the parish, provision may be made by the annual meeting
for due representation of the congregation of each place
of worship, or for the election of district church councils.[3]
The Rules also make provision for the establishment of
joint parochial church councils where there is more than
one parish in the area of a benefice, or benefices are held
in plurality, of team councils, and of group councils.[4]
Fuller details relating to elections by the annual meeting
will be found in the rules themselves.[5]

3. THE PAROCHIAL CHURCH COUNCIL

The council consists of all clerks in holy orders beneficed
in or licensed to the parish (including vicars in a team
ministry), any deaconess or lay worker licensed to the
parish, the churchwardens (if actual communicant
members of the Church of England and on the roll of the
parish), such readers whose names are on the roll as the
annual meeting determines, all persons on the roll who
are lay members of any deanery or diocesan synod or of
the General Synod—all these are ex-officio members; the
representatives elected at the annual meeting; and, if the
council so decides, co-opted members, in number not
exceeding one-fifth of the elected members, being either

1 Rule 38.
2 Rules 12 (1) (f) and 14.
3 Rule 16. See further p 116, below.
4 Rules 17, 17A and 17B.
5 Besides the rules already cited the reader is referred to rules 10, 10A,
  15, 20 and 39; and rule 36 concerning appeals.

in holy orders, or actual communicant members of the Church of England of seventeen years of age at least.[1] A member of the council may resign at will.[2]

The council must appoint a secretary, and meet at least four times a year. Provisions respecting the officers, meetings and proceedings of the council, and for a standing committee and other committees, are in Appendix II to the Rules.[3] These provisions may be varied by the council with the consent of the diocesan synod.[4]

The council is a body corporate; and any act of the council may be signified by an instrument executed pursuant to a resolution of the council, and signed (unless sealing is required) by the chairman and two members present when the resolution was passed.[5] But under the Corporate Bodies' Contracts Act 1960 it will be sufficient if a contract, required to be in writing but not under seal, is signed by any person acting under the council's authority; or, where it is not required to be in writing, if it is made by word of mouth by any person so acting.

The council has power to acquire land for ecclesiastical purposes or educational schemes, but subject to the consent of the diocesan board of finance (except in the case of a lease for a year or less), and the land vests in the diocesan board; and the same applies to personal property to be held on permanent trusts.[6] 'Educational schemes' are schemes for providing facilities for spiritual, moral and physical training, and the council may participate in

1 Rule 12. For the meaning of 'actual communicant member' see note 2 on the previous page.
2 Rule 40.
3 See p 209, below.
4 Rule 13.
5 Parochial Church Councils (Powers) Measure 1956, s 3.
6 Parochial Church Councils (Powers) Measure 1956, ss 5 and 6. The Council may not dispose of the property without the consent of the diocesan board.

such schemes with the consent of the diocesan education committee.

The particular functions of the council are dealt with in the appropriate parts of this book, especially in chapters 8 and 9. But it is convenient to notice here one or two enactments not otherwise mentioned which require consultation with the council in various contexts. There is, for example, Canon B 8 (replacing the Vestures of Ministers Measure 1964) which regulates the vestures that may be worn, and requires the minister to consult the council before changing the form of vesture in use, and ascertain that the change is acceptable. Under the Clergy (Ordination and Miscellaneous Provisions) Measure 1964 (section 11) the bishop must consult the council before issuing or refusing a licence to a clergyman authorising him to engage in certain trades or occupations. And the requirements relating to the forms of service must not be overlooked.[1]

1 See pp 47, 50, below.

CHAPTER FIVE

Churchwardens and Sidesmen

1. APPOINTMENT OF CHURCHWARDENS

The rules governing the appointment, admission and resignation of churchwardens are contained in the Churchwardens (Appointment and Resignation) Measure 1964.[1] There are to be two churchwardens in every parish, unless an existing custom provides for a different number.[2] Where there is more than one parish church by virtue of a pastoral scheme, there are to be two churchwardens for each church, but all will be churchwardens for the whole parish unless they arrange for separate duties.[3]

To be appointed a churchwarden a person must be twenty-one years of age, an actual communicant member of the Church of England unless the bishop otherwise permits, and either resident in the parish or on the electoral roll of the parish. He must have consented to serve before

1 The Measure is printed in full in the Appendix (p 224, below).
2 Churchwardens (Appointment and Resignation) Measure 1964, ss 1 (1) and 12 (2). The custom must have existed for at least forty years before 1 January 1965, when the Measure came into operation. Examples of customs under which there are more than two church-wardens are to be found at St Michael's, Cornhill, in the City of London (three) and at Hornsea, East Yorkshire, now called Humberside (four). In *R v Hinckley Inhabitants* (1810) 12 East 361, a custom to have one churchwarden only was upheld.
3 Pastoral Measure 1983, s 27.

he is chosen.[1] A woman may be appointed a church-warden.[2]

The churchwardens are to be chosen annually, not later than 30 April in each year, at a meeting of the parishioners. This means a joint meeting of persons on the church electoral roll, and of other persons resident in the parish and entered on a register of local government electors by reason of residence there. This meeting must be convened by the minister or the churchwardens, by a notice, signed by the minister or a churchwarden, stating the place, day and time of the meeting. The notice must be put on or near the main door of the parish church and of every other building in the parish licensed for public worship, for a period including the two Sundays before the meeting. The minister presides at the meeting, or, if he is absent, a chairman chosen by the meeting. The meeting can settle its own rules of procedure, and adjourn if necessary. The minutes of the meeting should be recorded by a clerk appointed by the meeting.[3]

The churchwardens are to be chosen by the joint consent of the minister and the meeting, if possible. This 'joint consent' will be given if one or more motions naming the churchwardens have been declared carried by the chairman, and the minister has announced his consent to the choice of any person named, either before the motion is put, or immediately after it is declared carried. If the minister and the meeting cannot agree on the choice of *both* churchwardens or if no or insufficient motions have been moved, one churchwarden is to be appointed by the minister and the other *elected* by the meeting. If

1 Measure of 1964, s 1. For the meaning of 'actual communicant member' see note 2, on p 35, above.
2 *Gordon v Hayward* (1905) 21 TLR 298.
3 Measure of 1964, ss 2, 3 and 4, and rule 11 of the Church Representation Rules.

there is no minister, both wardens will be elected by the meeting. And if at any time a casual vacancy occurs amongst the churchwardens (eg by reason of death) a person may be chosen to fill the vacant place in the same way as the warden he is replacing was chosen.[1]

Elections to the office of churchwarden are to be conducted, announced and notified in the same manner as all elections at annual meetings, as prescribed by rule 10 of the Church Representation Rules, except that everyone entitled to attend the meeting of parishioners other than the minister will be entitled to nominate and vote.[2] Appeals lie as laid down by rule 36 of the Rules.

The churchwardens are admitted to their office by the Ordinary or his substitute. They must appear before him and make and sign a declaration that they will faithfully and diligently perform the duties of their office.[3]

If a churchwarden ceases to be resident in the parish, and his name is not on the electoral roll of the parish, he vacates his office. A churchwarden may resign with the written consent of the minister and any other warden, by instrument in writing addressed to the bishop, who may accept the resignation or not.[4] Otherwise a churchwarden remains in office until his successor is admitted.[5]

---

1 Measure, s 2. But if there is an existing custom (as defined in note 2 on p 39, above) for churchwardens to be chosen in some other manner, it will hold good despite the Measure; except that where the custom has been for a warden to be chosen by the vestry, whether alone or jointly with someone else (eg the minister), the meeting of parishioners replaces the vestry for this purpose (s 12 (2)).
2 Church Representation Rules, rule 11.
3 Measure of 1964, s 7.
4 Ibid, ss 8 and 9.
5 Ibid, s 7 (2).

The Measure confers on the bishop of the diocese a power to supplement its provisions in various ways, and to remove difficulties.[1]

2. APPOINTMENT OF SIDESMEN

Any person whose name is on the electoral roll of the parish may be a sidesman.[2] The sidesmen are elected at the annual parochial church meeting in accordance with Rule 10 of the Church Representation Rules.[3]

3. DUTIES

The churchwardens are officers of the Ordinary, and they represent the whole of the parishioners, not merely those who are members of the Church of England. Their rights and duties are dealt with in the following pages.[4] They relate to the collection of alms, the maintenance of order, the allocation of seats, the parochial registers, the protection of church goods, by action, if necessary, and the guardianship of the interests of the church against certain forms of wrong-doing. It is the duty of the churchwardens to inform the bishop, or other Ordinary, of any neglect of duty or impropriety of conduct on the part of the incumbent or the officers of the church. With the incumbent and at least two other persons appointed by the

---

1 Measure of 1964, s 11. Special provision is made in respect of the guild churches in the City of London (s 10); as to these churches see note 2 on p 47, below.
2 Church Representation Rules, rule 9 (2).
3 And the minister has no special say in regard to their choice.
4 See especially chapters 8, 9 and 10; also Canon E 1.

council they form the standing committee of the council,[1] which has power to transact the business of the council between the meetings of the latter, and subject to its directions.

If there are special trust funds of which the church-wardens are the trustees, they continue to be such trustees, notwithstanding the financial powers of the council. But the Incumbents and Churchwardens (Trusts) Measure 1964 required the incumbent, churchwardens and par-ochial church council to inform the diocesan authority in writing of any ecclesiastical charitable trust (with some exceptions) held by the incumbent or churchwardens. The property is vested in the diocesan authority as custodian trustee, while the incumbent or churchwardens remain as managing trustee or trustees. But managing trustees may not sell, lease, let, exchange, charge or take legal pro-ceedings in respect of the property without the consent of the diocesan authority.[2]

When the profits of a benefice are sequestrated, for example when it becomes vacant, the churchwardens are often appointed sequestrators, and it will then be their duty to pay out of the profits of the benefice the remuner-ation of any clergyman appointed by the bishop to officiate during the vacancy, paying any balance left to the Church Commissioners.[3] If the bishop does not appoint a curate the churchwardens may (after appointment as seques-trators) employ one to perform the services. But the churchwardens, as such, have no right during a vacancy

1 If they are themselves members of the council.
2 Regarding the registration of religious charities under the Charities Act 1960 see the pamphlet RE 4R issued by the Charity Commission (57–60 Haymarket, London SW1). Parochial Church Councils are largely, but not entirely, exempted from registration (SI 1963/2074, Regs 1 and 2).
3 Endowments and Glebe Measure 1976, s 38.

to arrange for the performance of the services. They only have this right if they are appointed sequestrators, and they then act as the officers of the bishop.[1]

The Benefices (Sequestrations) Measure 1933 confers additional powers on sequestrators appointed to act during a vacancy. They may, with the approval of the bishop (or the archdeacon if the bishop has delegated his powers to him), provide for the care of the house of residence, garden and other land, and for payment for professional assistance if they need any in carrying out their duties; or grant a lease of the house or land.[2] Subject to the rights of an outgoing incumbent, they may sell the garden and other produce, when the proceeds will be part of the income of the benefice.[3]

The sidesmen originally performed the duty of presenting to the bishop all those in the parish, including the clergy, who had fallen short in what was required of them by the ecclesiastical law; but this duty in course of time fell on the churchwardens. Canon E 2 provides that 'It shall be the duty of the sidesmen to promote the cause of true religion in the parish and to assist the churchwardens in the discharge of their duties in maintaining order and

1 *A-G v St Cross Hospital* (1856) 8 De GM & G 38.

   In practice sequestrators are not now often appointed, and the bishop requests the churchwardens to arrange services. See note 3, below.

2 The consent of the Church Commissioners must be obtained as well as the authorisation of the bishop (Endowments and Glebe Measure 1976, s 38). And see s 68 of and Sch 7 to the Pastoral Measure 1983 as to the duties of sequestrators during a period of suspension under s 67 of that Measure.

3 An up-to-date review of the law and practice relating to sequestration, with suggestions for reform, is contained in paras 36–51 of the Report of the Working Party on The Work of Diocesan Registrars (GS 808, November 1987). Legislation is expected.

decency in the church and churchyard, especially during the time of divine service.' There is no limit to their number. In fact sidesmen are not appointed in every parish.[1]

1 'There is no foundation for the statement, which is as old as the seventeenth century, that "sidesman" in this sense is a corruption of "synods man".'—Oxford English Dictionary.

CHAPTER SIX

The Duties of the Incumbent and Rights of the Parishioners in relation to the Church Services

I. PUBLIC WORSHIP

One consequence of the establishment of the Church of England is that the incumbent of every parish is bound by law to provide services in the church; and the parishioners have a right to attend those services. Further, the forms of service which may be used are provided for by law. A series of Acts of Parliament, from the Act of Uniformity of 1662 onwards, and Measures of the National Assembly and the General Synod, have provided forms of service.[1] But these enactments were superseded by the Church of England (Worship and Doctrine) Measure 1974, and it is convenient to begin this chapter with an account of this Measure.

The Measure is almost solely an enabling one, conferring powers on the General Synod to act by Canon. There is a general power to make provision with respect to worship in the Church of England, and Canons may empower the Synod to approve, amend, continue or discontinue forms of service. The General Synod may make provision, by Canon or regulations thereunder, for any matter to which the rubrics in the Book of Common Prayer relate, except the publication of banns; and the

1 For an account of these the reader is referred to the fourth edition of this work, chapter 5 especially.

Canons and regulations have effect notwithstanding anything in the rubrics inconsistent with them. But the forms of service contained in the Book of Common Prayer are to remain available.[1]

The General Synod is required to provide by Canon that decisions as to which of the authorised forms of service are to be used in a church shall be taken jointly by the incumbent and the parochial church council, and Canon B3 accordingly so provides. In case of disagreement the forms in the Book of Common Prayer are to be used unless other authorised forms have been in regular use in the church for at least two of the four years immediately preceding the date of the disagreement, and the council resolves that those other forms shall be used (either exclusively, or as well as the prayer book forms). In the case of the occasional offices, however, other than the order of confirmation, the decision as to which form of service is to be used is to be the minister's; but if any person concerned objects beforehand to the form of service chosen, and he and the minister cannot agree on the question, it is to be referred to the bishop.[2]

The Synod has also made Canon B4, empowering the Convocations and the archbishops and bishops to approve

1 Church of England (Worship and Doctrine) Measure 1974, s 1. The Book of Common Prayer is the Book annexed to the Act of Uniformity 1662, as altered or amended by any Act or Measure. Any Canon or regulation as above will have effect notwithstanding any inconsistency with the rubrics (s 1 (2)). Canons under s 1 (1), and s 2 (1) referred to below, must be approved by a two-thirds majority of each House (ibid, s 3).

2 Church of England (Worship and Doctrine) Measure 1974, s 1 (3) and (4), and Canon B3. In the case of a guild church it will be the vicar and guild church council who are involved in the decision as to the forms of service to be used, other than for the occasional offices. As to these churches, see the City of London (Guild Churches) Acts 1952 and 1960: Halsbury, Vol 14, para 597.

forms of service for use when no provision is made by the Book of Common Prayer or under Canon, and Canon B5, empowering any minister to make and use minor variations in the authorised forms of service, and to use forms of service considered suitable by him on occasions for which no provision is made. Canon B5A enables the archbishops to authorise the use in draft form of forms of service in course of preparation, before a congregation of persons designated by the archbishop.

In the prayers for or referring to the Sovereign or Royal Family the names may be altered, or other alterations made, by Royal Warrant, and the prayers as altered are to be used.[1]

Another provision of the Measure relates to doctrine. Under it the Synod has made Canons with respect to the obligations of the clergy, deaconesses and lay officers of the Church to assent or subscribe to the doctrine of the Church and as to the forms of assent or subscription.[2]

A Canon, regulation, approval or the like, relating to forms of service, and a Canon with respect to doctrine, must receive the final approval of at least two-thirds of those present and voting in each House of the General Synod.[3] Moreover, any such Canon or regulation, any form of service or amendment approved, and any form of service or variation approved, made or used by virtue of the power given to the Convocations, bishops and ministers referred to above, must be neither contrary to, nor indicative of any departure from, the doctrine of the Church of England in any essential matter.[4] This means

1 S 1 (7).
2 S 2. Canon C15 sets out the Declaration of Assent, and Canons D2, E5, E8, G2 and G3 state the declarations to be made by deaconesses, readers, women workers and deputies to certain judicial officers.
3 S 3.
4 S 4.

the doctrine stated in Canon A5: 'The doctrine of the Church of England is grounded in the holy Scriptures, and in such teachings of the ancient Fathers and Councils of the Church as are agreeable to the said Scriptures. In particular such doctrine is to be found in the Thirty-nine Articles of Religion, the Book of Common Prayer, and the Ordinal.'[1]

Canons in accordance with the above provisions have been made by the General Synod. Canon B1 authorises the use of the forms of service contained in the Book of Common Prayer, the shortened forms of morning and evening prayer which were set out in the Schedule to the Act of Uniformity Amendment Act 1872,[2] the service authorised by Royal Warrant for use on the anniversary of the day of the Sovereign's accession, and any forms of service approved under Canon B2 or Canon B4. Canon B2 is merely an enabling Canon in the terms of sections 1 (1), 3 and 4 of the Measure of 1974 above cited. Canon B4 does little more than repeat the words of section 1 (5) (*a*) of the 1974 Measure given above, enabling the Convocations, archbishops and bishops to approve forms of service for use on occasions for which no provision is otherwise made, being forms which in 'both words and order' are 'reverent and seemly'. Canon B4A enables the Synod to approve new forms for the collects and Tables of Lessons. The Revised Tables of Lessons Measure 1922 authorised the use of a revised table contained in the Measure.

The General Synod has, under the Canons, authorised the use of alternative forms of service which are contained in the Alternative Service Book 1980.[3] The archbishops have authorised a special form of service for Remem-

1 S 5 (1).
2 Repealed by the Measure of 1974.
3 Authorisation is for a term of years—at present until the end of the year 2000.

brance Sunday, and the House of Bishops has commended forms of service of prayer and dedication after civil marriage, and services and prayers for Lent, Holy Week, and Easter.

Canon B5 authorises the minister in his discretion to make variations not of substantial importance in any authorised form of service according to particular circumstances, and (subject to any regulation by Convocation) to use on occasions for which no provision is otherwise made forms of service considered suitable by him. The variations and forms must be reverent and seemly, and of course neither contrary to, nor indicative of, any departure from the doctrine of the Church of England in any essential matter.

Under the Prayer Book (Versions of the Bible) Measure 1965, wherever in the prayer book a portion of scripture is set out and appointed to be read, said or sung, the minister may use in its place the corresponding portion in any version of the Bible for the time being authorised for the purpose by (now) the General Synod; but only with the agreement of the parochial church council, or, in the case of the occasional offices, if none of the persons concerned has objected beforehand. The Revised Psalter approved by the Convocations in October 1963 is deemed to have been authorised under the Measure, and thus may be used. Under this Measure, the use of the Revised and Revised Standard Versions of the Bible, the New English Bible, the 'Jerusalem Bible', the Good News Bible (Today's English Version) and, except in Prayer Book Communion Services, the New International Version Bible, has been authorised.

The General Synod, under Canon B6, and, subject to any directions of the Convocation, the Ordinary, may approve holy days additional to those appointed by the prayer book.

It should also be noticed that the Prayer Book (Further Provisions) Measure 1968 added at the end of the rubric in the prayer book headed 'The Order for Morning and Evening Prayer' a new paragraph as follows:

'Readers and such other lay persons as may be authorised by the Bishop of the diocese may, at the invitation of the Minister of the parish or, where the Cure is vacant, or the Minister is incapacitated, at the invitation of the Churchwardens, say or sing Morning or Evening Prayer (save for the Absolution); and in case of need, where no clerk in Holy Orders or Reader or lay person authorised as aforesaid is available, the Minister or (failing him) the Churchwardens shall arrange for some suitable lay person to say or sing Morning or Evening Prayer (save for the Absolution).'

There was also added, immediately after the Absolution, the following:

'If no priest be present the person saying the Service shall read the Collect for the Twenty-First Sunday after Trinity, that person and the people still kneeling.'

Canon E4 now provides for the functions of readers.

Section 4 of the Measure of 1968 gave the General Synod power to authorise rules for regulating the service when two holy days fall upon the same day, and on similar occasions; and rules for this purpose were authorised by the General Synod in February 1973.[1]

1 These remain valid notwithstanding the repeal of the 1968 Measure (Church of England (Worship and Doctrine) Measure 1974, Sch 3). For further legal detail regarding the authorised services the

To pass now to the requirements as to when the services are to be held, Canon B11 provides that as a general rule morning and evening prayer shall be said or sung in every parish church at least on all Sundays and other principal feast days, Ash Wednesday and Good Friday. It also requires the minister, and any other clergy licensed in the parish, 'being at home and not otherwise reasonably hindered', to resort to the church in the morning and evening on all other days, and, warning being given to the people by the tolling of the bell, to say or sing the common prayers and on the appointed days the litany. The services must be said or sung distinctly, reverently and in an audible voice. Canon B6 enumerates the principal feasts. The bishop has under Canon B11 the power to dispense with the reading of morning and evening prayer, but apparently retains the power under section 80 of the Pluralities Act 1838 to enforce two services on Sundays; and this, with certain limitations, even where there is more than one church or chapel in the benefice. The same provision empowered the bishop to enforce the preaching of a sermon at morning and evening service on Sundays, but Canon B11 provides that a sermon shall be preached at least once each Sunday.

Regarding churches which are not parish churches, and buildings licensed for public worship, the bishop may, under Canon B11A, direct what services are to be held.

The bishop may, under Canon B11, if he is satisfied that there is good reason to do so, authorise the minister of any parish church to dispense with the reading of morning and evening prayer, or either, on any Sunday, or on Ash Wenesday, Good Friday, or any principal feast

reader may refer to Opinions p 136, and, for a practical guide, Public Worship in the Church of England (1986) issued by the General Synod (Church House Bookshop, Great Smith St, London SW1P 3BU).

day. But before authorising the minister to dispense with morning or evening prayer on Sundays for more than three months the bishop must consult the parochial church council (or two members nominated by it for the purpose); and the bishop must not use his power so as to cause the church to be no longer used for public worship. The bishop's power extends to parish centres of worship designated under section 29 of the Pastoral Measure 1983.[1]

It has been held, as indicated at the beginning of this chapter, that 'the inhabitants of a parish have a legal right and a reasonable expectation that divine offices should be performed in their own church'.[2] And by section 27 (5) of the Pastoral Measure 1983, where a parish has more than one parish church by reason of a pastoral scheme or otherwise, the parishioners have the same rights of worship in each of the parish churches. If the minister neglects to perform the services, an action for damages will not lie against him;[3] and the appropriate course would be to consider proceeding under the Ecclesiastical Jurisdiction Measure 1963, or the Incumbents (Vacation of Benefices) Measure 1977.[4]

If a person is ill or in danger of death in the parish, the minister, on being informed, must go to such person and exhort, instruct and comfort him. A form of service for the visitation of the sick is contained in the prayer book. Likewise the minister should administer the communion privately to such a person, or anyone unable to go to church, and desiring to receive it.[5]

1 Canon B11A.
2 *Bishop of St David's v Baron de Rutzen* (1861) 7 Jur NS 884 at 887.
3 *Williams' Case* (1592) 5 Co Rep 72b.
4 See p 32 above, for the former, and p 29, above for the latter Measure.
5 Canon B37. Under s 1 of the Extra-Parochial Ministry Measure 1967 and Canon C8 a minister (including a curate) may perform offices and services at the home of someone on the electoral roll of

Section 1 of the Act of Uniformity of 1551, which imposed a duty on members of the Church of England[1] to attend service on Sundays and holy days, was repealed by the Statute Law (Repeals) Act 1969.

It was held in *Taylor v Timson*[2] that the Act of Uniformity, by imposing a duty to attend divine service, conferred a correlative general right to attend the parish church. In the modern case of *Cole v Police Constable 443A*[3] the plaintiff, who was attending a service at Westminster Abbey not on a Sunday or holy day, was ejected by a constable on the instructions of the dean. The Abbey is a royal peculiar and it was held that the plaintiff, who did not claim to be a parishioner, could properly be excluded from a service there. In the course of the judgments the view was expressed that the right of a parishioner to attend church was an old common law right not depending on the statutory duty to attend church;[4] and presumably this was the view of the law taken when section 1 of the Act of Uniformity was repealed, as it can hardly have been intended to abolish by implication the right of a parishioner to attend public worship in his parish church.[5]

A parishioner having the right to attend church has a

---

but not resident in the parish, as for a parishioner, and without the consent of the minister of the other parish. But there must be present only members of the family or household. And see p 69, below as to the marriage of housebound or detained persons.

1 For what constitutes membership of the Church of England see *Re Perry Almshouses* [1898] 1 Ch 391, and *Re Allen* [1953] Ch 810.
2 (1888) 20 QBD 671.
3 [1937] 1 KB 316.
4 Per GODDARD J, at p 333.
5 The Act of Uniformity of 1551 was no doubt repealed as an enactment 'no longer of practical utility', to quote a part of the long title of the repealing Act; and see the First Report of the Law Commission on Statute Law Revision (Cmnd 4052 of 1969), pp 1 and 35.

right of action in the ordinary courts of law against anyone who prevents him from so doing.[1]

Finally, it is appropriate to end these paragraphs relating to public worship on an ecumenical note. The Sharing of Church Buildings Act 1969 and the Sharing of Church Buildings Measure 1970 authorised the making of agreements for the sharing of churches and other buildings by Churches of different denominations.[2] Now the Church of England (Ecumenical Relations) Measure 1988 authorises the making of Canons to enable members of a church designated by the archbishops to take part in public worship according to the forms of service and practice of the Church of England; to enable clerks in holy orders, deaconesses, lay workers and readers to take part in worship according to the forms of service and practice of a church so designated; and to enable a place of worship of the Church of England to be made available for the conduct of such worship. There are restrictions regarding services of holy communion and marriage. Canon B43 has been made under this Measure.

2. HOLY COMMUNION

By Canon B14 holy communion is to be celebrated on all Sundays and principal feast days and Ash Wednesday, except for some reasonable cause approved by the bishop.[3] By Canon B12, no person is to consecrate and administer it 'unless he shall have been ordained priest by episcopal ordination' in accordance with Canon C1; and no person is to distribute it unless ordained in accordance with that

1 *Taylor v Timson* (1888) 20 QBD 671.
2 Forms of sharing agreement are given in the Encyclopaedia of Forms and Precedents (5th edn), Vol 13, p 158 et seq.
3 Leavened or unleavened bread may be used (Canon B17.2).

Canon or otherwise authorised by Canon, or specially
authorised by the bishop under regulations made by the
General Synod.[1] Subject to the general directions of the
bishop the epistle and gospel may at the invitation of the
minister be read by a lay person. Similar authority is given
to a deaconess by Canon D1.[2] Canon B15 lays down that
it is the duty of all who have been confirmed to receive
holy communion regularly, and especially at Christmas,
Easter, and Whitsun.[3]

Reservation is permissible.[4]

All parishioners who are confirmed members of the
Church of England have the right to be admitted to
partake of the holy communion.[5] And Canon B15A
requires that there be admitted to holy communion,
besides confirmed members of the Church of England,
those ready and desirous to be confirmed, or otherwise
episcopally confirmed; baptised persons who are communicant members of other Churches subscribing to the
doctrine of the Holy Trinity; other baptised persons authorised to be admitted under regulations of the General

1 Regulations made by the Convocations with the concurrence of
 the House of Laity were on 13 January 1970 declared an Act of
 Convocation in each province, and continue in force as if made by
 the General Synod (Synodical Government Measure 1969, Sch 4,
 para I (1)). See the regulations reproduced on p 154 of the current
 code of Canons.
2 See p 29, above.
3 As to administration to the sick, see p 53, above.
4 *Re Rector and Churchwardens of Bishopwearmouth v Adey* [1958] 3 All
 ER 441 (reservation for the sick); *Re St Nicholas, Plumstead* [1961]
 1 All ER 298 (reservation to meet the necessities of the parish); *Re
 St Peter and St Paul, Leckhampton* [1968] P 495 (reservation in
 general). A faculty may have to be obtained sanctioning the means
 to be used.
5 S 8 of the Sacrament Act 1547 required the minister not to deny the
 communion 'without lawful cause': see *Jenkins v Cook* (1876) 1 PD
 80. The rubric in the text now states what is a 'lawful cause'.

Synod; and any baptised person in immediate danger of death.[1] This is subject to the rubric, which is now as follows:

'If a Minister be persuaded that any person who presents himself to be a partaker of the Holy Communion ought not to be admitted thereunto by reason of malicious and open contention with his neighbours, or other grave and open sin without repentance, he shall give an account of the same to the Ordinary of the place, and therein obey his order and direction, but so as not to refuse the Sacrament to any person until in accordance with such order and direction he shall have called him and advertised him that in any wise he presume not to come to the Lord's Table; Provided that in case of grave and immediate scandal to the Congregation the Minister shall not admit such person, but shall give an account of the same to the Ordinary within seven days after at the latest and therein obey the order and direction given to him by the Ordinary; Provided also that before issuing his order and direction in relation to any such person the Ordinary shall afford to him an opportunity for interview.'[2]

Canon B17 requires the churchwardens to provide a sufficient quantity of bread and wine.

1 The Admission to Holy Communion Measure 1972 provided that the rubric at the end of the Confirmation Service, that no-one shall be admitted to the communion until confirmed, or ready and desirous to be confirmed, was not to prevent the provision by Canon and regulations of the General Synod for the admission to holy communion of other baptised persons.
2 Substituted for the second and third paragraphs of the introductory rubric to the communion service by s 3 of the Prayer Book (Miscellaneous Provisions) Measure 1965.

3. BAPTISM

The requirements for the baptism of infants are now in Canons B21 to B23. If the requirements are met, the minister must baptise the child.[1] If he declines or unduly delays, the parents or guardians may apply to the bishop for his directions.

Canons B22 and B23 provide that at least a week's notice should normally be given. There should usually be at least three godparents, two of the same sex as the child and one of the opposite sex; but if three 'cannot conveniently be had', one godfather and one godmother will suffice. Parents may be godparents for their own children if the child has at least one other godparent. The godparents are to be persons who have been baptised and confirmed, and who will 'faithfully fulfil their responsibilities both by their care for the child committed to their charge and by the example of their own godly living'. But the minister may dispense with the requirement of confirmation in any case in which in his judgment there is need to do so.

The minister is to instruct the parents or guardians that the same responsibilities rest on them as are required of the godparents.

The essentials of baptism are the invocation of the Holy Trinity and the use of water. It should properly be administered by a priest, but it may be administered by a deacon, and it has always been the law that in case of necessity a layman or woman may baptise.[2] Under Canon D1, a deaconess may be authorised by the bishop to

---

1 If the parents live outside the boundaries of his cure, and neither of them has his or her name on the church electoral roll, the minister should first seek the good will of the minister of the parish where they live.

2 *Escott v Mastin* (1842) 4 Moo PCC 104; *Cope v Barber* (1872) LR 7 CP 393 at 402.

baptise in the absence of the minister. No fee may be demanded by the minister, clerk, or any other person for the administration of baptism.[1] Nor may a minister refuse to baptise a child on the ground that conditions of his own imposing, for example as to doctrine, have not been complied with.[2]

Canon B21 provides that it is desirable to administer baptism on Sundays at public worship 'when the most number of people come together', to witness it. And by Canon B22 no minister, on being informed of the weakness or danger of death of any infant within his cure, shall if he is desired to do so refuse or delay to go and baptise the child. Canon B24 provides for the baptism of persons of riper years and able to answer for themselves.

A register book of public and private baptisms, in the form required by the Parochial Registers and Records Measure 1978, must be provided by the parochial church council; if there is more than one parish church, one for each church. The person performing the ceremony in a parish church, or elsewhere in the parish if he is a minister of the parish, must as soon as possible after doing so enter the required particulars and sign the register. If a person who is not a minister of the parish performs the ceremony elsewhere than in a parish church, he must as soon as possible send to the incumbent or priest in charge a certificate as to when and where the ceremony was performed, and containing the required particulars. The incumbent or priest in charge enters the particulars in the register, adding the words 'According to the certificate of   received by me on the   day of   '.[3] Errors may be corrected within one month

1 Baptismal Fees Abolition Act 1872, s 1.
2 See *Bland v Archdeacon of Cheltenham* [1972] Fam 157, p 123, below.
3 See s 2 (3) of the Measure as to baptisms performed in an extra-parochial place, and s 5 as to baptisms in a church or chapel not belonging to a parish.

of their discovery by an entry in the margin, made in the presence of, and attested by, either or both of the parents of the child, or, in case of the death or absence of both, the churchwardens, and signed and dated by the person making the entry. The original entry should not be altered. The Baptismal Registers Measure 1961 provides for the annotation (in the form prescribed) of an entry in respect of a person who, since baptism, has been legitimated and whose birth has been re-registered in the register of births; and for any certificate of baptism to show the annotation. It also provides for the giving, on request, in *any* case, of a 'short certificate of baptism', which, in the case of a legitimated person as above, will show the surname as that recorded in the annotation.

Where a child has been adopted *after* baptism, arrangements have been approved by the archbishops under which the adopting parents may send the full certificate of entry in the baptismal register for registration in a Diocesan Register of the Baptism of Persons Subsequently Adopted. A special certificate of baptism will then be issued, bearing the new name or names.[1]

4. MARRIAGE

All persons who are legally entitled to marry have, as a general rule, the right to be married in the church or chapel of the parish or district where one of them resides, or which is the usual place of worship of one of them.[2]

---

1 Christian names given in baptism may not legally be changed except by the bishop at confirmation, by Act of Parliament, Royal Licence, or on adoption.
2 A person's 'usual place of worship' is the church on the electoral roll of which his name is entered (Marriage Act 1949, s 72).

This is probably so even if neither party has been baptised; but the marriage would be after banns, not by licence.[1] The minister is bound to perform the ceremony, and if, without good reason, he refuses to do so, he is liable to censure in the ecclesiastical courts.[2]

Where by reason of a pastoral scheme or otherwise there is more than one parish church in a parish or benefice, marriages may be solemnised in any of the churches, and the bishop may give directions with respect to the publication of banns and solemnisation of marriages in them.[3]

The parties will not be legally entitled to marry if they are within the prohibited degrees of relationship.[4] These extend to relationship by the half-blood,[5] by illegitimacy,[6] and by adoption.[7] Under the Marriage (Enabling) Act 1960, replacing, with widened scope, previous statutory exceptions to the prohibited degrees, a marriage between a man and a woman who is the sister, aunt or niece of a

1 Opinions, p 91.
2 *Argar v Holdsworth* (1758) 2 Lee 515. It is questionable whether he is liable to an action for damages in the ordinary courts (*Davis v Black* (1841) 1 QB 900); or to be indicted (*R v James* (1850) 3 Car & Kir 167).
3 Pastoral Measure 1983, s 27 (5) and Sch 3, para 14; Marriage Act 1949, s 23. S 20 of the Marriage Act 1949 enables the bishop to license 'public chapels' for the publication of banns and solemnisation of marriages, eg a Chapel of Ease, or the place of worship of a conventional district, even though unconsecrated.
4 See Marriage Act 1949, Sch 1, Pt I, as amended by Marriage (Prohibited Degrees of Relationship) Act 1986 (p 62, below) and Canon B31.
5 Marriage Act 1949, s 78 (1), ('brother' and 'sister'). See also Canon B31.
6 *R v Brighton Inhabitants* (1861) 1 B & S 447; *Restall (otherwise Love) v Restall* (1929) 45 TLR 518.
7 See s 39 of the Adoption Act 1976, under which an adopted child is, broadly speaking, to be treated in law as a child of a marriage.

former wife of his (whether living or not), or was formerly the wife of his brother, uncle or nephew (whether living or not), is lawful.

The Marriage (Prohibited Degrees of Relationship) Act 1986 has made further inroads into the table of prohibited degrees by making lawful under certain circumstances marriage with a person related through a former spouse. Schedule 1 to the Act adds new Parts I and II to Schedule 1 to the Marriage Act 1949, listing the relationships involved.

Both parties must have reached the age of sixteen,[1] and if one or both of them is under eighteen and not a widow or widower, the minister must not marry them if the parents or guardian, as the case may be, refuse their consent.[2] They must also have complied with the provisions requiring banns, a licence, or a superintendent registrar's certificate, set out below.

If one of the parties has been previously married, and the marriage has been dissolved on any ground, and the former husband or wife is still living, the minister may perform the ceremony, or not, according to his discretion. But he is not compelled to solemnise the marriage, or to permit it to take place in the church of which he is minister.[3] The same rule holds as regards marriages under the Marriage (Prohibited Degrees of Relationship) Act 1986,[4] and, it appears, those under the Marriage (Enabling) Act 1960, except perhaps where the former spouse has died.

1 Marriage Act 1949, s 2.
2 Marriage Act 1949, s 3, and Family Law Reform Act 1969, s 2. See, further, note 2 on p 66, below, as to whose consent is required.
3 Matrimonial Causes Act 1965, s 8.
4 See s 3.

Banns

Banns of marriage are to be published in the church of the parish where the parties reside, or if they reside in different parishes, then in both those parishes; they may, in addition, be published in a church which is the usual place of worship[1] of either party.[2]

The parties can be married only in a church in which their banns have been published, so that the effect of the law as above stated is as follows. If both parties dwell in the same parish, and wish to be married in the parish church, their banns will be published there. If they dwell in different parishes, their banns will be published in the churches of both those parishes, and they may be married in either of those churches. If they wish to be married in a church which is the usual place of worship of either or both of them, but neither of them dwells in the parish served by that church, their banns must be published *both* in that church *and* in the church of the parish in which they dwell (or, if they dwell in different parishes, in the churches of both those parishes).[3]

1 See note 2 on p 60, above.
2 A marriage made lawful by the Marriage (Prohibited Degrees of Relationship) Act 1986, where the relationship is one specified in Part II of Sch 1 to the Marriage Act 1949 added by the 1986 Act (see p 62, above) must not proceed by banns (1986 Act, Sch 1, para 3).
3 As to the position where there is more than one parish church, see p 61, above. And see para 14 of Sch 3 to the Pastoral Measure 1983.
   It follows from the above statement that a foreigner not residing in the United Kingdom cannot marry by banns; and even if a foreigner does reside here the Legal Advisory Commission of the General Synod recommends that the marriage should be by licence, to enable the Diocesan authorities to make sure that the legal requirements of his country are being observed. See Opinions, p 92; and 'Suggestions for the guidance of the clergy' referred to in note 2 on p 73, below.

The parties intending to be married should give to the minister of each church where they wish their banns to be published, at least seven days before the first day of intended publication, a notice in writing, dated the day of delivery of the notice, containing their christian names and surnames and addresses, and the time during which each has been living at his or her place of residence.[1] Unless such a notice is delivered, the minister is not compelled to publish the banns. But he may do so. If, however, he publishes the banns without such a notice, and the parties are not in fact entitled to have their banns published, he is liable to ecclesiastical censure.[2]

A clergyman should always inquire whether there is any impediment to an intended marriage.[3] And it is his duty, at any rate if there is any circumstance which ought to make him suspicious, to satisfy himself that there is no

1 Marriage Act 1949, s 8. What is meant is the 'known and acknowledged names of the parties as those which their relations and friends are presumed to be the best acquainted with' (Hammick, *Law of Marriages*, 2nd edn (1887), p 70). See *R v Billinghurst Inhabitants* (1814) 3 M & S 250, where a man whose baptismal name was Abraham Langley was married by banns in the name of George Smith, by which name he had been known in the parish where he was married for three years, and it was held that the marriage was valid. In *Dancer v Dancer* [1949] P 147, the woman had been born 'Knight' but brought up 'Roberts', and on her asking the vicar which name to give he said 'Roberts'. The court upheld the marriage, as there was neither fraud nor concealment. But in *Chipchase v Chipchase* ([1939] P 391 and [1942] P 37), it was finally held that, where a woman (whose first husband was presumed dead) had been married after publication of banns in her maiden name, the second 'marriage' was void, since, although she had been known for at least two years by her maiden name, she was married in that name because 'it served to conceal—or at any rate not to emphasise—the fact that she was already married'. The second 'husband' knew all the facts.
2 See *Wynn v Davies* (1835) 1 Curt 69, pp 83, 84.
3 Canon B33.

false statement in the particulars given to him, and that there is no legal impediment. If he finds that a false statement has been made, he should decline to publish the banns.[1]

The banns must be published in the form prescribed in the rubric to the marriage service,[2] or that in the Alternative Service Book, on three Sundays (not necessarily successive Sundays, and not necessarily on the same Sundays if they are published in different churches), and at the morning service, or if there is no morning service at the evening service.[3]

The parochial church council must provide a proper banns book, marked and ruled in the manner directed for the register book of marriages. The banns must be published from this book and not from loose papers, and after each publication the entry must be signed by the minister or by someone under his direction.[4]

Banns must in general be published by a clerk in holy orders, but a deaconess may be authorised to publish them.[5] When a clergyman is not officiating at the service at which it is usual to publish banns, they may be published by a clergyman at some other service at which

---

1 *Priestley v Lamb* (1801) 6 Ves 421; *Nicholson v Squire* (1809) 16 Ves 259 at 261; *Sullivan v Sullivan* (1818) 2 Hag Con 238 at 253.
2 The form 'I publish the Banns of Marriage between [A. B., Bachelor] whose name is on the Electoral Roll of [this Parish]' may be used in the usual place of worship.
3 But see below as to publication when a clergyman is not officiating. The Legal Board, in their Thirty-fifth Annual Report (CA 1471), gave it as their opinion that banns may be called immediately before the offertory sentences at an early communion service in the church of a parish forming one of several parishes served by one priest who, with his bishop's permission, does not hold matins or evensong every Sunday in that particular church.
4 Marriage Act 1949, s 7; and see Canon F11.
5 See p 29, above.

banns may lawfully be published; or by a deaconess or lay person during the course of a public reading authorised by the bishop of a portion or portions of the service of morning or evening prayer, such public reading being at the hour when the service at which it is usual to publish banns is commonly held (unless the bishop authorises otherwise); and the incumbent (or some other clergyman nominated by the bishop) must have made, or authorised, the requisite entry in the banns book. A person who has published banns in accordance with this provision is to sign the banns book.[1]

Any person may 'forbid the banns' (that is, publicly declare that the marriage ought not to take place) on the ground that there is a legal impediment to the marriage (eg that one party is already married). If one of the parties is under eighteen, and not a widower or widow, his or her parent or guardian may forbid the banns on the ground that consent to the marriage is refused, in which case the publication is void.[2]

If the marriage does not take place within three calendar months after the date of the last publication, the banns must be published again three times.[3]

1 Marriage Act 1949, s 9, and Canon D1. Canons E4 and E7 provide for the publication of banns by lay readers.
2 Ibid, s 3 and Second Schedule. Broadly, if both parents are living either may dissent from the marriage, unless they are divorced or legally separated, in which case the parent having custody may dissent; if one parent is dead, the surviving parent of the guardian, if any, may dissent; if both parents are dead, any guardian may dissent. In the case of an illegitimate person, the mother, or, if she is dead, the guardian appointed by her, may dissent. But there are also special cases where the consent required will not be that of the parent or guardian, eg when the party is a ward of court, or the local authority has assumed parental rights under Part I of the Child Care Act 1980. See Opinions, p 89.
3 Marriage Act 1949, s 12.

The minister of the church where the parties are to be married must in all cases, before performing the ceremony, obtain a certificate of due publication of banns signed by the minister of any other church where they have been published (or by another clergyman nominated by the bishop).[1]

Licence

A licence is a dispensation from the publication of banns, addressed to the parties intending to marry, and to the minister. Authority to grant an ordinary, or 'common', licence is vested in the bishops, who delegate authority to certain of the clergy (called surrogates) appointed by the chancellor in each diocese.

Parties wishing to be married by licence must apply to a surrogate. One of them must swear before him that there is no legal impediment to the marriage, and that one of the parties has had his or her usual place of residence[2] within the parish in which the marriage is to be solemnised, for a period of fifteen days immediately preceding the granting of the licence, or that the church at which the marriage is to be solemnised is the usual place of worship of one of them. If either of the parties is under eighteen, and not a widower or widow, oath must also be made that the requisite consents have been obtained.[3] A licence will then usually be granted as a matter of

1 Ibid, s 11. If one of the parties resides in Scotland or any part of Ireland, a certificate of due publication there may be accepted. If one of the parties is in the navy and borne on the books of one of HM's ships at sea, the banns may be published on three successive Sundays at morning service on board ship, and a certificate issued and accepted accordingly. (Marriage Act 1949, ss 13 and 14).
2 The deposit of a suitcase does not satisfy this requirement.
3 Marriage Act 1949, s 16. As to consents, see note 3 on the previous page.

course, but the issue of the licence is entirely at discretion;[1] and a licence will not normally be granted where neither party has been baptised.[2]

On production of the licence it is the duty of the minister of the church mentioned therein to solemnise the marriage; and the burden of ascertaining that the facts stated by the parties are true lies on him who grants the licence, and not on the officiating minister. But if there are circumstances which clearly show to the latter that the bishop or other person granting the licence has been misled, it will doubtless be his duty to refuse to celebrate the marriage; and if he has reasonable grounds for suspecting fraud in the parties, he may delay the ceremony in order to make inquiries.[3]

If the marriage does not take place within three calendar months after the granting of the licence, the licence is void.[4]

Besides these 'common', or ordinary, licences, special licences may be granted by the Archbishop of Canterbury,[5] which enable the parties to be married at any place and time convenient to them.

A 'caveat' may be entered against the granting of a licence by anyone who, if the marriage had been intended to take place after publication of banns, might have forbidden the banns.[6]

---

1 *Prince of Capua v Count de Ludolf* (1836) 30 LJPM & A 71n.
2 See p 61, above, and note 1 on that page.
3 *Argar v Holdsworth* (1758) 2 Lee 515; *Tuckness v Alexander* (1863) 32 LJ Ch 794 at 806.
4 Marriage Act 1949, s 16.
5 Under the Ecclesiastical Licences Act 1533.
6 See p 66, above.

Registrar's Certificate

A marriage may also be solemnised in church by a clergy-man on production of a certificate granted by the super-intendent registrar, but only with the consent of the minister of the church.[1] The certificate is granted by the superintendent registrar of the district in which the parties reside, on twenty-one days' notice being given to him. If the parties reside in different districts, the certificates of the superintendent registrars of both districts must be obtained. The certificate may authorise the solemnisation of the marriage in the usual place of worship of one of the parties, wherever it may be situate.[2] Under the Mar-riage Act 1983 a person confined to his house through illness or disability, or who, with certain qualifications, is in hospital or in prison, may, on the registrar's certificate, be married where he 'usually resides', the place being specified in the certificate.

A 'caveat' may be entered against the granting of the certificate.[3] The marriage must be celebrated within three calendar months of the giving of the notice, not the granting of the certificate.[4]

The Marriage Ceremony

The marriage must be solemnised by a clerk in holy orders of the Church of England; and a marriage solemnised by a deacon, including a woman deacon, is a valid marriage.[5]

1 Marriage Act 1949, s 17.
2 Ibid, s 35, amended by the Marriage Act 1949 (Amendment) Act 1954.
3 Marriage Act 1949, s 29.
4 Ibid, s 33.
5 *R v Millis* (1844) 10 Cl & Fin 534. HL, pp 666, 667; *Beamish v Beamish* (1861) 9 HL Cas 274, 325. Some doubt is felt as to whether a deacon *ought* to solemnise a marriage because of uncertainty as to whether

It must take place in church,[1] between the hours of eight in the forenoon and six in the afternoon.[2] The ceremony must be according to the form for the solemnisation of matrimony in the prayer book, or according to a form approved under the Prayer Book (Alternative and Other Services) Measure 1965; and it must be performed in the presence of two witnesses.[3] The clergyman solemnising the marriage must immediately afterwards enter the required particulars in duplicate register books, and the entries must be signed by him, by the parties, and by two witnesses.[4] Any mistake in the entry may be corrected within one month by making an entry in the margins of both books, signed and dated, in the presence of the parties, who must also sign. The original entry should not be crossed out. If either of the parties is absent or dead, the correction should be made in the presence of, and signed by, the churchwardens, or the superintendent registrar and two witnesses.[5]

---

a deacon has authority to pronounce a blessing, a question now under consideration by the House of Bishops. The Legal Advisory Commission has given full consideration to this question.

1 Unless under the Marriage Act 1983, as to which see the text above. The Marriage Act 1949 (ss 18 to 21) provides for marriages during disuse of churches whilst being rebuilt or repaired, and for licensing of chapels by the bishop (and see note 3 on p 6, above); and ss 68 to 71 for marriages in naval, military and Air Force chapels. See also Cripps, pp 541, 542 and 553–557, for the law generally as to the churches and chapels in which marriages may be solemnised.

2 Marriage Act 1949, s 4.

3 Ibid, s 22.

4 Marriage Act 1949, ss 53 and 55. If the marriage is under the Marriage Act 1983 it must be registered in the register of any church or chapel in the parish or extra-parochial place where it is solemnised, or, if none, in any adjoining parish. An incumbent may, if necessary, lend his register for the purpose (Marriage Act 1983, Sch 1, para 17). The incumbent must make quarterly returns to the superintendent registrar.

5 Marriage Act 1949, s 61. The power does not apply where it is

When a marriage has been solemnised in the presence of a superintendent registrar, a clergyman may, if he thinks fit, and the parties so request, read or celebrate the marriage service in respect of them; but no entry is to be made in the marriage register.[1]

When Marriage Void

Non-compliance with the various legal requirements set out in the preceding pages will not necessarily render the marriage void. A marriage will be void only if the parties knowingly and wilfully marry—

    (a) in a church or other building where banns may not be published, ie where marriages may not lawfully be solemnised;[2] or

    (b) when the ceremony is performed by a person not in holy orders; or

    (c) without due publication of banns,[3] or obtaining a licence, or a registrar's certificate given after due notice; or

    (d) after banns have been forbidden; or

    (e) after the expiration of three months from the last day of publication of banns, or the date of the licence, or of the notice to the registrar, as the case may be; or

---

sought to strike out an entry on the ground that the marriage was void, or to make a note in the margin to that effect. *Dinizulu v A-G and Registrar-General* [1958] 3 All ER 555.

1 Ibid, s 46, and Canon B36.

2 Apart from the cases under the Marriage Act 1983 (p 69, above).

3 As an example of this, it was held in *Hooper (Orse Harrison) v Hooper* [1959] 2 All ER 575, that a 'marriage' in a Church of England church in Baghdad, without publication of banns, was void.

(f) if the marriage is on the registrar's certificate, in any place other than the building specified therein.[1]

The absence of witnesses,[2] or the performance of the ceremony outside the prescribed hours,[3] or departure from the order of service laid down, will not render the marriage void.[4]

It is, moreover, important to note that, for the marriage to be void within the above rules, both parties must be aware of the defect, whatever it is, at the time of the ceremony, and deliberately marry notwithstanding their knowledge.[5] Guilty knowledge or fraud on the part of one only of the persons contracting is never sufficient to avoid the marriage,[6] and there must be a design on the part of both to circumvent the law, for example to conceal identity by securing publication of banns in a false name.[7] Not even statements as to name and residence made when applying for a licence and false to the knowledge of both parties will cause the marriage to be void.[8] Even if the marriage is performed by someone not a clergyman, it will stand unless the parties are aware of the deception.[9]

1   Marriage Act 1949, ss 25 and 49.
2   *Wing v Taylor* (1861) 2 Sw & Tr 278 at 286.
3   See *Catterall v Sweetman* (1845) 1 Rob Eccl 304 at 317.
4   In the Australian case of *Quick v Quick* [1953] VLR 224 (cited in the Law Quarterly Review for July 1955), where the woman had changed her mind when the man was putting the ring on her finger, and had run out of the building, it was held that the marriage was complete when the parties had exchanged their promises.
5   *Greaves v Greaves* (1872) LR 2 P & D 423.
6   *Templeton v Tyree* (1872) LR 2 P & D 420.
7   See p 64, above.
8   *Bevan v M'Mahon* (1861) 2 Sw & Tr 230; *Plummer v Plummer* [1917] P 163; *Puttick v A-G* [1979] 3 All ER 463.
9   Sir Wm SCOTT (as he then was) in *Lord Hawke v Corri* (1820) 2 Hag Con 280 at 288. See also *R v Millis* (1884) 10 Cl & Fin 534, HL, and *Beamish v Beamish* (1861) 9 HL Cas 274, on the question of the validity of marriages not celebrated by a clergyman of the Church

If in any legal proceedings the validity of the marriage is subsequently called in question, no evidence can be given that the parties were not in fact residing within the parish as required by law (or in the registration district stated in the notice to the registrar), or that their names were not on the electoral roll of the parish where they were married, as the case may be.[1] The effect of this is that once the marriage has been celebrated, its validity is not affected by non-residence or absence of enrolment.[2]

5. BURIAL

A parishioner, wherever he may die, has the right to be buried in the churchyard, or other burial ground, of his own parish;[3] a non-parishioner, whose name is on the church electoral roll of the parish, has the right to be buried in the churchyard or other burial ground of the parish;[4] and a non-parishioner has the right to be buried in the churchyard or other burial ground of the parish

---

of England. In the latter case the bridegroom, who was a clergyman, himself purported to celebrate the marriage, and it was held void.

1 Marriage Act 1949, ss 24 and 72.
2 See further on the matters dealt with in this and the next section, 'Suggestions for the guidance of the clergy relative to the duties imposed upon them by the Marriage and Registration Acts', issued (1989) by the Registrar General, 10 Kingsway, London WC2.

Under the Provisional Order (Marriages) Act 1905, as amended, the Home Secretary can make an order, in the case of any marriage which appears to be invalid on account of some informality, removing the invalidity, or any doubt as to the validity, and relieving ministers of any liability.
3 *Ex parte Blackmore* (1830) 1 B & Ad 122. 'Although to speak of the deceased as having a right of burial involves some laxity of language, the expression is convenient and sanctioned by usage' (Halsbury, Vol 10, para 1118).
4 Church of England (Miscellaneous Provisions) Measure 1976, s 6 (1).

where he dies.[1] Other persons may not be buried there without the consent of the incumbent, who must have regard to any general guidance given by the parochial church council.[2]

A person's right to burial is merely, as expressed by LORD STOWELL,[3] a right 'to be returned to his parent earth for dissolution'; and he has no right to be buried in any particular manner or in any particular place in the churchyard, unless he has a faculty for, or a prescriptive or statutory[4] right to, the use of a particular vault or place. Moreover, section 8 of the Faculty Jurisdiction Measure 1964 provided that any exclusive right to a burial space shall cease one hundred years from the passing of the Measure unless a faculty is issued after the passing of the Measure (which cannot itself be for more than one hundred years). Subject to the faculty jurisdiction the decision of matters relative to burial rests with the incumbent.

By the Births and Deaths Registration Act 1926, section 1,[5] the minister is bound, under penalty, not to perform the burial until he receives a certificate of the registration of the death from the registrar, or a coroner's order; but he may proceed with the burial if he is satisfied, by a

1 Canon B38. See the Pastoral Measure 1983, Sch 3, para 15 as to the burial rights in new or altered parishes resulting from pastoral schemes or orders.
2 Measure of 1976, s 6 (2). The incumbent's decision may not be reviewed by the consistory court (*Re St Nicholas's, Baddesley Ensor* [1982] 2 All ER 351). A reasonable charge might be made, as a contribution to the maintenance of the churchyard.
    For the rules relating to burial in the church itself, reference must be made to Cripps, p 567; and as to the right of burial in a ground provided by a burial authority, see p 113 below.
3 In *Gilbert v Buzzard* (1820) 3 Phillim 335, at 352, 353.
4 See s 9 of the Consecration of Churchyards Act 1867.
5 Amended by the Births and Deaths Registration Act 1953, Sch 1.

written declaration made by the person procuring the disposal of the deceased, that a certificate of the registrar or order of the coroner has in fact been issued, although it has not been delivered to him. Within ninety-six hours of disposing of the body, the minister is to deliver to the registrar a notification of the date, place, and means of disposal of the body (section 3). Further, he must not bury a still-born child until he has received a certificate given by the registrar under section 11 of the Births and Deaths Registration Act 1953, or a coroner's order (section 5). In the case of a burial under the Burial Laws Amendment Act 1880, which is dealt with below, the person upon whom the duties imposed by sections 1 and 3 are cast is the relative or other person having charge of or being responsible for the burial, and not the minister (section 12).

Due notice of an intended burial must be given to the minister: that is, notice must be given to him so that he has due time to make preparations for the burial, having regard to his occupations and convenience.[1] Such warning having been given, the minister is bound to bury the body according to the form of service provided for the burial of the dead in the prayer book, or in the alternative form in the Alternative Service Book 1980.[2] For failure to perform this duty he is liable to ecclesiastical censure, and also to proceedings in the ordinary courts.

The prayer book service must not be used if the deceased person had not been baptised (this does not mean baptised according to the rites of the Church of England);[3] or if he had 'laid violent hands' on himself.[4] This phrase does not appear to have obtained interpret-

1 *Titchmarsh v Chapman* (1844) 1 Rob Eccl 175; Canon B38.
2 See p 49, above.
3 Rubric before the burial service.
4 Rubric before the burial service.

ation in a judicial decision; but Burn, in his work on Ecclesiastical Law,[1] says that the rubric does not exclude from burial in the ordinary manner persons who are idiots, lunatics, or otherwise of unsound mind, children under the age of discretion, or those who kill themselves by accident. The practice is for the prayer book service to be used if the person killed himself while not responsible for his action.[2] Even where that service cannot be used, the minister must allow burial in the churchyard.[3] There may be used the form of service approved under section 13 of the Burial Laws Amendment Act 1880, mentioned below; or the form of service in the Alternative Service Book.

It is illegal, subject to what follows, for anyone not a minister of the established Church to read, or to assist in reading, the burial service in a consecrated burial ground, as it is indeed illegal, apart from the provisions about to be mentioned, for any unauthorised person to perform any service in consecrated ground.[4] A deaconess, a reader, and a lay worker, may, however, be authorised by the bishop to bury the dead, or read the burial service before, at or after a cremation, with the good will of the persons responsible.[5]

Further, the Burial Laws Amendment Act 1880 provided for the reading of a service other than that in the prayer book. Anyone having charge of the burial of a deceased person may give notice in writing that it is

1 Vol 3, p 654; see on this point *Clift v Schwabe* (1846) 3 CB 437.
2 The Suicide Act 1961, which repealed the Interments (felo de se) Act 1882, abrogated the rule of law that suicide was a crime.
3 *R v Taylor* (1721) 7 Davy 278 MS, cited in *Andrews v Cawthorne* (1745) Willes 536. A verbatim copy of the report of *R v Taylor* is contained in the Appendix to Prideaux, p 548.
4 *Johnson v Friend* (1860) 6 Jur NS 280; *Wood v Headingley-cum-Burley Burial Board* [1892] 1 QB 713.
5 See Canons D1, E4 and E7.

intended that the burial shall take place without the service prescribed in the prayer book; and if the burial is to take place in a churchyard, forty-eight hours' notice must be given, and it must state the proposed time of burial. If this is inconvenient, another may be arranged. The burial may then take place without any service at all; or some 'Christian and orderly religious service' may be read at the grave.[1] The service may be read by any person who is invited by those in charge of the burial to read it, and all persons are to have a right of access to the churchyard for the service.

The minister must, as soon as possible after the burial, enter particulars in the register of burials, to be provided by the parochial church council, and sign the register.[2] Any error may be corrected within one month of its discovery by an entry in the margin made in the presence of and attested by two persons who were present at the burial or by the churchwardens, and signed and dated by the person making the entry.[3] The original entry should not be altered.

Under section 12 of the Burial Laws Amendment Act 1880, a clergyman may read the burial service in any unconsecrated burial ground, but he cannot be compelled to do so. Further he may, under section 13, in any case where it is unlawful to use the burial service according to

1 'Unitarians are commonly, and always have been considered as forming a part of the Christian community.' (MAULE J, in *A-G v Shore* (1843) 11 Sim 592 at 619.)
2 Parochial Registers and Records Measure 1978, ss 1 and 3. If there is more than one burial ground in use a register must be provided for each. See s 3 (2) as to burial in an extra-parochial place, and s 5 as to burial in a church or chapel not belonging to a parish. The provisions for registration do not apply to a burial under the Cemeteries Clauses Act 1847, or in a cemetery under s 214 of the Local Government Act 1972.
3 Measure of 1978, s 4.

the rites of the Church of England, and in any other case at the request of the person having charge of the burial, use a form of service approved by the Ordinary.

Under Canon B38 the minister's duty to bury a corpse, as stated at the beginning of this section, extends to ashes after cremation; and, except for good and sufficient reason, ashes should be interred or deposited by a minister in consecrated ground. Section 11 of the Cremation Act 1902 provided that the incumbent of a parish is not under any obligation to perform a funeral service before, at, or after the cremation of a deceased person, within the ground of a burial authority; but on his refusal to do so, any clergyman may perform the service in such ground, on being requested so to do by the person having charge of the cremation or by the burial authority, and on obtaining the permission of the bishop. A faculty will be granted in a proper case for the interment of an urn containing cremated remains below the floor of a church.[1] The interment of ashes in a closed churchyard is not prohibited by the Burial Acts.[2]

6. CUSTODY AND CARE OF REGISTER BOOKS

The incumbent has the custody of the register books of baptisms, confirmations, banns of marriage, marriages, burials or services; during a vacancy, the churchwardens have the custody.[3] The registers and other records in parochial custody are to be inspected periodically, at the cost of the parochial church council, by persons appointed by the bishop, and reports sent to him and the council.

1 *Re Kerr* [1894] P 284.
2 See *The Churchyards Handbook* (note 1, p 109, below) on the disposal of ashes after cremation.
3 Parochial Registers and Records Measure 1978, s 6. This is so although they may belong to the parochial church council.

Register books and records that have not been in use for a hundred years are to be deposited in the diocesan record office, unless the bishop authorises retention in parochial custody. Later registers, not in use, may also be deposited with the consent of the parochial church council.

Custody involves responsibility for safe-keeping, care, and preservation, and the bishop may issue directions on these matters, to be carried out at the cost of the parochial church council. The registers and records will normally be kept in the parish church or other place of worship. Provision is made for making register books and records available for exhibition or research, and an incumbent, priest in charge or churchwarden having custody of a register of baptisms or burials must allow searches to be made in them at reasonable hours, and give copies of entries, certified under his hand, on payment of any prescribed fee.[1]

1 See ss 16–18 and s 20 of the Measure.

CHAPTER SEVEN

The Organist, Choir, Parish Clerk and Sexton

I. THE ORGANIST AND THE CHOIR

An organist was long said to be 'a person unknown to ecclesiastical law, either as an official of the church or as a servant of the parish'.[1] But his existence has been tardily recognised by the Church of England (Legal Aid and Miscellaneous Provisions) Measure 1988, which authorises Canons to 'make provision with respect to the appointment of persons to act as organists and choirmasters (by whatever name called) and with respect to the termination of such appointments.' Canon B 20 accordingly now provides that the incumbent, with the agreement of the parochial church council, has the right to appoint the organist or choirmaster (or 'choir director') on such terms as they think fit, and to terminate the appointment. In the case of termination, however, the archdeacon may dispense with the agreement of the council if he considers the circumstances so require. Further, the incumbent is to pay 'due heed' to the organist's advice and assistance in the choosing of the music. The final responsibility in these matters rests, however, with the incumbent, who has the control of the manner in which divine service is to be performed. Canon B 20 also provides that it is the incumbent's duty to ensure that only such chants, hymns, anthems and other settings

1 Sir Travers Twiss, quoted in Blew's *Organs and Organists*, p 16.

are chosen as are appropriate, in their words and music, to worship and prayer, and to the congregation assembled.

A written agreement, to which the incumbent, the council and the organist are parties, should be made. It should provide for such matters as salary, duties, use of the organ, holidays and termination eg one or three months notice on either side. The old rule was that, if no stipulation as to notice had been made, three months notice would be reasonable.[1]

The council must maintain the organ in proper repair.

In pursuance of his right to direct the manner of the performance of divine service, the incumbent may appoint singers to form a choir.[2]

2. THE PARISH CLERK AND SEXTON

The offices of parish clerk and sexton are both known to the common law and are of ancient origin; and the office of parish clerk is indeed a temporal office coming within the jurisdiction of the ordinary courts.

The chief duty of the parish clerk used to be to lead the laity in the performance of their part in divine service. It is said that originally all parish clerks were in holy

---

1 See Blew, p 58.
2 A bequest to the vicar and churchwardens 'for the benefit of the choir' is a good charitable gift (*Re Royce* [1940] Ch 514).

A form of agreement for the appointment of an organist (and choir director) has been issued by the Royal College of Organists and other bodies, with the approval of the Legal Adviser to the General Synod. The Incorporated Society of Musicians has also issued the 'Organist's guide to employment', (which includes recommendations as to salaries and fees). These, and other information on church music, may be obtained from the Royal School of Church Music, Addington Palace, Croydon CR9 5AD. A form of agreement may also be found in the Encyclopaedia of Forms and Precedents (5th edn, Vol 13, p 79).

orders,[1] and it has been expressly enacted that a clergyman
may hold the office.[2] The duties of the sexton, on the
other hand, are of a more manual nature: they include the
care of the church and churchyard, the digging of graves,
the care of the ornaments in the church, and other things.
It was long ago held that the office of sexton could be
held by a woman.[3]

The parochial church council has power jointly with
the incumbent to appoint and dismiss the parish clerk and
sexton or any persons performing or assisting to perform
their duties. The council and incumbent jointly also determine their salaries and the conditions of tenure of their
offices and of their employment.[4] They are also entitled
to fees under the Parochial Fees Order 1988.[5] In ancient
parishes a parish clerk may have a freehold for life in his
office,[6] and a sexton may also by custom hold his office
for life,[7] but it is clear that the council and the incumbent
now have power to appoint to the offices on whatever
terms they think fit. A written agreement should therefore
be made, stating the terms of appointment.[8]

The parish clerk is growing obsolete, both in name and
function, and the designation 'sexton' is also tending to
disappear. A frequent practice is to appoint a person (who
may be called a 'verger') to carry out the duties of the
sexton (especially to take care of the church and its furniture and the churchyard) and to assist the minister and

1 Gibson's *Codex Juris Ecclesiastici Anglicani* (1713) p 240: 'Parish
   Clerks were heretofore real Clerks.'
2 Lecturers and Parish Clerks Act 1844, s 2.
3 *Olive v Ingram* (1739) 2 Stra 1114.
4 Parochial Church Councils (Powers) Measure 1956, s 7; Canon E 3.
5 See Appendix, p 236, below.
6 *R v Warren* (1776) 1 Cowp 370.
7 *R v Dymock (Vicar and Churchwardens)* [1915] 1 KB 147.
8 The Encyclopaedia of Forms and Precedents (5th edn, Vol 13, p 78)
   gives a form of agreement with a 'verger or parish lay administrator'.

churchwardens in carrying out their duties. The law gives authority over such a person to the council and incumbent jointly.[1]

---

1 Parochial Church Councils (Powers) Measure 1956, s 7 (iii), and Canon E 3.

CHAPTER EIGHT

The Finance of a Parish

I. FUNDS COLLECTED IN THE CHURCH

The rubric at the end of the offertory sentences in the service of holy communion provides that during the reading of the sentences the deacons, churchwardens, or other fit persons, are to receive the alms of the people in a decent basin.[1] It is also customary for a collection to be made at matins and evensong, and at other services held in the church and elsewhere, or for money to be placed in envelopes. Since the passing of the Church of England (Legal Aid and Miscellaneous Provisions) Measure 1988 (section 13) it is no longer necessary to distinguish between collections at a service of holy communion and collections made at other services in church. In regard to the money collected, and money given generally in church, as, for example, money placed by visitors in an alms box, or given by the audience at a musical recital in the church, the council and the incumbent acting jointly

---

1 See *Cope v Barber* (1872) LR 7 CP 393; and *Howell v Holdroyd* [1897] P 198.

The 'Offertory' is the name of that portion of the Communion Service which immediately follows the rubric 'Then shall the Priest ... begin the Offertory ...' The word is often improperly applied to the collection of alms made at this point, and even to the alms themselves. See, for an exhaustive discussion of many matters connected with the Offertory, *Harrison on Rubrics* (1845), pp 277 et seq.

have together complete authority to determine the objects to which the money so collected or given shall be allocated.[1] If they cannot agree, the matter should be referred to the bishop for his determination.[2] When a collection is taken for a special object, the object should be made known beforehand, and the money collected should of course be applied accordingly.[3]

Where there is a custom to give the money collected on Easter Day to the incumbent, the latter will have a right to the money so collected, for his personal use. Though the matter is not free from doubt, it seems to be the better opinion that the clergy have no general legal right to Easter offerings, but in order to establish the right in a particular parish a custom to give them to the incumbent must be proved.[4] Easter offerings, if given to the incumbent by way of augmentation of his stipend, are assessable to income tax.[5]

The council may appoint one or more of its members to act as treasurer, solely or jointly.[6] The churchwardens may be appointed to act as joint treasurers, and if no other person is appointed they will, if members of the council, be treasurers ex officio. In practice, therefore, the church-wardens, acting on behalf of the council, will often have the handling of the money collected in church, as they

1 S 7 (iv) of the Parochial Church Councils (Powers) Measure 1956; and see Canon F 10.
2 S 9 (3) of the Measure of 1956, and Canon F 10.
3 *Marson v Unmack* [1923] P 163. The rule extends to, for example, a 'retiring collection' made at a funeral service, at the request of the family, for a particular charity. The intention should be made plain, and the money collected (or a proportion of it, if that is the intention) paid by the council's treasurer to the charity.
4 *R v Reeves* (1733) 2 Eag & Y 55.
5 *Blakiston v Cooper* [1909] AC 104.
6 Church Representation Rules, Appendix II, para 1 (e).

did before the reforms of 1921;[1] but they hold it at the disposal of the incumbent and council.

2. FUNDS OTHERWISE COLLECTED

If the incumbent holds a service or meeting elsewhere than in the church, a collection may be made for any object desired by him, and the money collected must be applied to the object for which the collection was expressly or impliedly made. Neither the churchwardens nor the council have any authority over the money so collected, except in one case: if a collection is made for 'church purposes', that is, for a purpose connected with the fabric, furniture or services of the church, so that if it had been made before 1921 the churchwardens could have administered the money, then the council has, under the Measure of 1956, sole authority to dispose of the money.[2]

The same reasoning applies to the disposal of the funds collected at any meeting or entertainment held by any person other than the incumbent. If the money is collected for a 'church purpose' as described above, the council has authority over its disposal. If it is collected for any other purpose, then the person in charge of the meeting or

1 See p 5, above.
2 Parochial Church Councils (Powers) Measure 1956, s 4 (1) (ii) (a). And see *Marson v Unmack* [1923] P 163.

The council has not been given by the current legislation any powers in regard to the administration of ecclesiastical charities. Section 7 of the Measure of 1921, which gave it power to appoint trustees of these, and to see their accounts, was dropped from the Measure of 1956.

See p 43, above, as to charitable trusts of which the incumbent or churchwardens are trustees.

Regarding house-to-house collections, street collections, and appeals outside the parish by the clergy or other parochial authorities, see Opinions, p 23.

entertainment must, according to the ordinary law relating to trustees, apply the money to the object for which it was collected, and neither the incumbent, the churchwardens, nor the council have as such any right to the money.

3. CHURCH RATES

By section 7 (ii) of the Parochial Church Councils (Powers) Measure 1956, the council is given power to make a voluntary church rate for any purpose connected with the affairs of the church. The council has in this respect inherited the old powers of the vestry,[1] and the rate affords a means of informing each member of the church what he may reasonably be expected to contribute towards the fund required; but it is thought that such a rate is seldom levied in practice, and that it is more usual to raise money by other means at the disposal of the council. It also has power to raise loans, and a limited ability to give security.[2]

4. CHURCH EXPENSES

By section 7 (i) of the Measure of 1956 the parochial church council is given power to frame an annual budget of moneys required for the work of the church and to take the necessary steps for the raising and allocating of such moneys. In particular, it has under section 4 the former powers and duties of the churchwardens with regard to the care and maintenance of the fabric and ornaments of the church and the care of the churchyard,

---

1 S 4 (1) (i) of the Measure of 1956. (Since the Compulsory Church Rate Abolition Act 1868, payment of such a rate cannot be enforced in the courts.)
2 See Opinions, p 87; and *Re St Peter, Roydon* [1969] 2 All ER 1233.

and under section 7 power jointly with the incumbent to determine the salaries of the parish clerk and sexton.

The church council, then, has authority to determine what are the necessary and proper expenses of the church, and has power to raise the money required to meet these expenses. Any member of the council (including, of course, the incumbent and churchwardens) may at a meeting of the council, subject to due notice, propose specified expenditure; and, if it relates to the 'maintenance of the work of the church', the council may sanction the expenditure and approve means for raising the money.[1]

The council has, however, not only complete authority to sanction any expenditure, but it is also in certain cases bound to provide for necessary expenses. It has inherited the duties and liabilities of both the vestry and the church-wardens in most matters relating to church expenses. The several matters to which these duties and liabilities relate will be dealt with later under their appropriate headings.[2]

Section 8 of the Measure of 1956 requires the council to furnish to the annual parochial church meeting accounts, made up to 31 December immediately preceding the meeting, which are to set out the council's income and expenditure during the year; and to supply a statement of the funds and property, if any, remaining in the council's hands at the date of the account. The accounts and state-ment must be audited and copies fixed on or near the church door at least seven days before the meeting. They are then submitted to the meeting for its approval; and, if approved, they are to be signed by the chairman of the

1 The council could apply to the local authority (including a parish or community council) for a contribution under s 137 of the Local Government Act 1972.
2 See chapters 9, 11 and 12; and chapter 6 as to the provision of register books.

meeting and 'published' by the council.[1] Accounts of any trusts administered by the council are to be laid before the diocesan board of finance annually.

5. FEES

The Ecclesiastical Fees Measure 1986 governs the matter. The Schedule to the Parochial Fees Order 1988, printed in the Appendix to this book,[2] fixes the fees payable to the incumbent, parish clerk, sexton, and parochial church council in respect of baptisms, marriages, burials, the erection of monuments,[3] and searches in church registers.

The fees are recoverable by proceedings in the county court.[4]

---

1 See rule 8 of the Church Representation Rules.
2 SI 1988/1327. See p 237, below.
3 'Monument' includes 'headstones, crosses, kerbs, borders, vases, chains, railings, tablets, flatstones, tombstones or monuments or tombs of any other kind.'
4 See the Legal Officers' Fees Order 1986 (SI 1986/1144), the Legal Officers (Annual Fees) Order 1987 (SI 1987/1296) and the Ecclesiastical Judges and Legal Officers (Fees) Order 1987 (SI 1987/1297) as to fees payable to ecclesiastical judges and legal officers.

CHAPTER NINE

The Fabric, Ornaments and Furniture
of the Church

I. THE FABRIC OF THE CHURCH

The freehold of the church is as a general rule, by the common law, vested in the incumbent.[1] Where there is a lay rector the freehold is in him, but 'this naked and abstract right carries with it ... no right of possession, the latter being in the incumbent';[2] and in certain cases an aisle of the church, or a chapel, may be vested in a private person. Apart from these exceptional cases, the freehold is in the incumbent.[3] Under section 1 of the Faculty Jurisdiction Measure 1964 a faculty may be granted, on the application of the incumbent or the parochial church council, vesting in the incumbent (or lay rector) any privately owned building or structure forming part of and physically connected with the church. Reasonable steps must be taken to communicate with the owner or supposed owner of the building; and either these must be shown to have been unsuccessful, or the owner, or

---

1 Where the right of presentation is suspended, the freehold is vested in the bishop.
2 COCKBURN CJ, in *Griffin v Dighton* (1863) 33 LJQB 29.
3 When land on which a church or other place of worship is built is held on lease, the leasehold interest may be enlarged into a freehold in accordance with the provisions of the Places of Worship (Enfranchisement) Act 1920 (extended to ministers' houses by s 40 of the Leasehold Reform Act 1967).

person reasonably claiming rights of ownership or possession, must have consented to the vesting.

The incumbent has the right to the possession of the keys of the church, and he may refuse access to all persons, including the churchwardens, except at proper times and for proper purposes determined by him.[1] The churchwardens have a right to enter the church at proper times for the performance of their duties,[2] and the parishioners have a right to resort to their parish church to attend divine service.[3] If the incumbent refuses access to the church for these purposes a complaint may be made to the Ordinary, but in the meantime the directions of the incumbent must be obeyed. If he persists in refusing access, he may be proceeded against in the ecclesiastical court.[4]

It was the duty of the parishioners under common law to maintain their parish church in repair,[5] though the duty is now a moral one only.[6] It was the duty of the churchwardens to see that any necessary repairs were executed. The liability to repair the chancel was, however, on the rector (whether clerical or lay), unless there was a custom for the parishioners to repair it.[7]

In 1921 the duties and liabilities of the churchwardens relating to the care, maintenance, preservation and insurance of the fabric of the church were transferred to

1 *Ritchings v Cordingley* (1868) LR 3 A & E 113.
2 *Ritchings v Cordingley*, above.
3 *Taylor v Timson* (1888) 20 QBD 671. See chapter 6.
4 *Bellars v Geast* (1741) Rothery's Precedents No 157, p 77.
5 *Gosling v Veley* (1853) 4 HL Cas 679. And see Prideaux, p 120.
6 Phillimore, p 1419.
7 *Hawkins v Rous* (1695) Holt KB 139. In the City of London, by particular custom, the parishioners repair both church and chancel (*Ball v Cross* (1689) Holt KB 138). See note 2 on p 47, above, as to guild churches; and p 103, below, as to private chapels etc.

the parochial church council.[1] It is now therefore the duty of the council to see that the fabric of the church is maintained in a proper state of repair, and to obtain the funds necessary for the purpose. To do this they have the power to levy a voluntary church rate or to take any steps they may deem expedient for raising the money required.[2]

As to the chancel, the Ecclesiastical Dilapidations Measure 1923 relieved incumbents of the obligation to repair and insure, providing that the chancel should be repairable and insurable in the same manner as the remainder of the church.[3] It was only the *incumbent* who was relieved of the duty to repair. Others such as lay rectors were enabled to compound their liability. And section 39 of the Endowments and Glebe Measure 1976 transferred to parochial church councils liability arising from the ownership of glebe or of tithe rentcharge extinguished by the Tithe Act 1936 and held by Queen Anne's Bounty.[4] The Chancel Repairs Act 1932 provided for proceedings by the parochial church council in the county court to enforce the repair of a chancel.

The diocesan synod is required to establish a scheme for the inspection of all churches in the diocese at least once in every five years.[5] The archdeacon may require the council to have the church inspected by an architect in accordance with the scheme if it has not been inspected

1 See now the Parochial Church Councils (Powers) Measure 1956, s 4 (1) (ii) (*b*).
2 If they cannot raise the money, they will be excused from performing their duty, *Millar and Simes v Palmer and Killby* (1837) 1 Curt 540.
3 S 52, amended by the Ecclesiastical Dilapidations (Amendment) Measure 1929, s 18.
4 See Halsbury's Laws, Vol 14, para 1100, et seq. for a fuller account of the law.
5 Inspection of Churches Measure 1955, and s 9 of Church of England (Miscellaneous Provisions) Measure 1978. See definition of 'church' in note 2 on p 117, below.

for five years; and if the council defaults for three months
the archdeacon may, with the consent of the bishop,
arrange for the inspection. The cost of inspection will fall
on the fund created under the scheme. Under Canon F18
the archdeacon, 'in person or by the rural dean', is to
survey the churches and churchyards in his jurisdiction
at least every three years.

Local authorities have power to contribute to the cost
of the repair or maintenance of buildings of architectural
or historic interest, and to pay the cost of repairing,
maintaining, winding and lighting public clocks.[1]

2. THE ORNAMENTS AND FURNITURE OF THE CHURCH

The goods, ornaments and furniture of the parish church
are vested in the churchwardens for the use of the parishioners, and devolve from time to time upon the successive holders of the office. For this purpose the
churchwardens are looked upon as a quasi-corporation,[2]
and they may sue and be sued in respect of the church
goods.[3] When goods or ornaments have been placed in
the church, however, and devoted to its use, they are
under the control of the incumbent and, as we have seen
above, he may keep the keys of the church. Nothing
contained in the Parochial Church Councils (Powers)

---

1 The principal enactments are the Local Authorities (Historic Buildings) Act 1962 and s 46 of the Public Health Acts Amendment Act
   1890.
2 *Fell v Official Trustee of Charity Lands* [1898] 2 Ch 44. The churchwardens are not a corporation for the purpose of holding land,
   except by a particular statute (see eg 9 Geo 1, c 7, s 4, since repealed),
   and in the City of London (*Warner's Case* (1619) Cro Jac 532).
3 One churchwarden cannot sue alone (*Fowke v Berington* [1914] 2 Ch
   308).

Measure 1956 affects the property of the churchwardens in the goods and ornaments of the church.[1]

It was the ancient duty of the churchwardens to provide, at the charge of the parish, all the ornaments and fittings necessary for the due performance of divine service and the sacraments in the parish church. This duty was transferred by the legislation of 1921 to the parochial church council.[2] The Canons require the following articles to be provided: a font with a cover, a holy table,[3] communion plate and linen, an alms basin, surplices for the minister, reading desks and pulpit, seats for the people, at least one bell to ring to service, bibles and prayer book for the minister, a service book, with cushion or desk, for the communion table, an alms box, register books of baptism, banns, marriage, burials and confirmations, and a register book of services in which is to be recorded every service of public worship, with the name of the officiating minister, the preacher (if someone else), the number of communicants and the amount of the collection (and if desired notes of significant events).[4]   Canon B31

1 S 4 (1) (ii).
2 Not expressly, but this seems to have been the effect of what is now s 4 (1) (ii) (*a*) and s 7 (i) of the Measure of 1956; and Canon F14 so provides.
3 Which may be movable or immovable, and of wood, stone or other suitable material. (Holy Table Measure 1964, repealed by the Church of England (Worship and Doctrine) Measure 1974. See Canon F2.) It need not resemble a domestic table (*Re St Stephen Walbrook* [1987] 2 All ER 578).
4 Canons F1 to 12. Register books for baptisms and burials are required by s 1 of the Parochial Registers and Records Measure 1978. The Marriage Act 1949 contains the requirements about the banns book (s 7) and the register books for marriage, which latter are to be provided in duplicate and by the Registrar General (ss 54 and 55).

   See p 78, above as to the custody and care of the registers.
   The Local Government (Records) Act 1962 empowers local auth-

requires a table of the prohibited degrees of marriage to be provided, and 'publicly set up'.

Beside the ornaments which are strictly necessary, the use of others is helpful and fitting in the performance of divine services, and many of these are usually to be found in churches. The introduction and use of these ornaments will be permitted provided that they are consistent with and subsidiary to the services. An account of the law governing the use of such ornaments must be sought elsewhere.[1]

Canon F17 requires the minister and churchwardens to keep a full record of the lands, goods and other possessions of the church, in accordance with instructions and forms prescribed by the General Synod.[2]

It was formerly the duty of the churchwardens to maintain the fittings of the church in repair, at the cost of the parish. The liability for the 'care, maintenance, preservation and insurance' of the goods and ornaments of the church was, however, like that for the repair of the fabric, transferred to the council.[3]

The requirement that the council is to submit to the annual parochial church meeting, for its approval, a report on the fabric, goods and ornaments of the church, has already been mentioned.[4] This, however, is perhaps the place to draw attention to the fact that the Town and Country Planning (Control of Advertisements) Regulations 1969 to 1974 apply in general to church notice

---

orities to purchase or accept the gift or deposit of records, and to contribute to the expense of taking care of records, and other expenses in relation to them. 'Records' includes parish registers.

1 See, for example, Prideaux, pp 56–89; Cripps, chapter XII.
2 A combined Terrier and Inventory is obtainable from Church House Publishing.
3 Measure of 1956, s 4 (1) (ii) (*b*).
4 See p 34, above.

boards which are visible from outside the building. The boards must, among other things, be kept in a clean and tidy condition.[1]

3. FACULTIES

A parish church 'belongs not to any one generation, nor are its interests and condition the exclusive care of those who inhabit the parish at any one period of time. It is in entire comformity with this aspect of the parish church that the law has forbidden any structural alteration to be made in it, save those which are approved by a disinterested authority in the person of the Ordinary.'[2] 'The contents of a church—the furniture and ornaments—are equally placed by law under the care of the Ordinary.'[3] Before, therefore, any alteration in the fabric or furnishings of the church can be made, and before any of the existing fittings or ornaments can be removed, or disposed of,[4] or any new fittings or ornaments placed in the church, it is necessary, strictly speaking, to have the permission of the Ordinary, such permission being given by means of the grant of a faculty by the chancellor of the diocese,

1 SI 1969/1532, 1972/489, and 1974/185.
2 Lord PENZANCE in *Nickalls v Briscoe* [1892] P 269 at 283.
3 Memorandum on the law of faculties by Sir Alfred B. Kempe, printed as appendix to Report of Archbishops' Ancient Monuments (Churches) Committee 1914.
4 This is so even though the church has been declared redundant (*Re West Camel Church, Re Yatton Church* [1979] 2 All ER 652). The parochial church council must consent to a disposal: *Re St Mary's Broadwater* [1976] 1 All ER 148. A memorandum on the 'Improper Removal of the Contents of Churches not Declared Redundant' has been drawn up by the Legal Advisory Commission (LAC (89) 3).

or, in minor cases, an informal licence;[1] or by means of the certificate described below.[2]

It has not in the past been the practice to require applications to be made for permission in respect of small matters such as hassocks or prayer books, or the execution of minor current repairs. Such matters have been left to the discretion of the incumbent and churchwardens. But a stricter view tends to be taken today; and inquiry of the Diocesan Registry, or the Diocesan Advisory Committee for the Care of Churches, should be made in any case of the least doubt.

Canon F13 lays down that it is the 'duty of the minister and churchwardens, if any alterations, additions, removals or repairs are proposed to be made in the fabric, ornaments, or furniture of the church, to obtain the faculty or licence of the Ordinary before proceeding to execute the same';[3] and that a record of those made is to be kept in a book to be provided for the purpose. The incumbent and churchwardens are the usual persons to petition for a faculty, but a petition may be presented by any parishioner and therefore the parochial church council may now petition for a faculty.[4] The granting of a faculty lies

1 The bishop may by himself, or with the chancellor, dispose of a faculty case, if the letters patent appointing the chancellor so provide (Ecclesiastical Jurisdiction Measure 1963, s 46).
2 Under s 6 of the Faculty Jurisdiction Measure 1964 the bishop may order than an unconsecrated building licensed for public worship shall be subject to the faculty jurisdiction. And unconsecrated land within the 'curtilage' of a church is also subject to the jurisdiction (s 7). See *Re St John's Church, Bishop's Hatfield* [1967] P 113, *Re Christ Church, Chislehurst* [1974], 1 All ER 146, and *Re St Mary Magdalene, Paddington* [1980] 1 All ER 279.
 See generally *Faculty Jurisdiction of the Church of England,* by G. H. Newsom (1988), for a full treatment of the subject.
3 Subject to the procedure by certificate mentioned on p 99, below.
4 *Re St Paul's Covent Garden* [1974] Fam 1; in *Re St James's, Bishampton* [1961] 2 All ER 1, the Minister of Aviation petitioned for a faculty

entirely within the judicial discretion of the Ordinary, and the consent of neither the incumbent[1] nor the church-wardens,[2] nor the parishioners,[3] is strictly necessary to the making of the grant; but any of these may oppose the grant of a faculty, and their views (especially those of the incumbent) are entitled to the greatest consideration.[4] The parochial church council has the right to be heard in a faculty case,[5] and here again in practice the consent of the council will usually have to be obtained because it will provide the necessary funds, unless they are obtained from a private benefactor. Under the Faculty Jurisdiction Measure 1964, the archdeacon,[6] and any person whose name is on the electoral roll, though not residing in the parish, is deemed to have an interest in faculty proceedings; and may therefore intervene.

This Measure also provides that the court may decree the issue of a faculty subject to a condition requiring the work authorised thereby to be carried out under the supervision of the archdeacon or some other person appointed by the court; or it may direct the issue to the archdeacon of a faculty in default of the incumbent and churchwardens carrying out the work.

---

for an alteration to a church tower close to an airfield.

As to fees, see note 4 p 89, above.

1 *Rugg v Kingsmill* (1867) LR 2 PC 59; *Re St Paul's, Covent Garden*, above.

2 *St Anne's, Limehouse (Rector) v St Anne's, Limehouse, Parishioners* [1901] P 73.

3 *Nickalls v Briscoe* [1892] P 269.

4 See *Re St Thomas's, Lymington* [1980] 2 All ER 84 as to the rights of parishioners.

5 *St Magnus etc Parochial Church Council v Chancellor of London Diocese* [1923] P 38, per SANKEY J, at p 45.

6 He should normally signify his view: see *Re St Mary's, Westwell* [1968] 1 All ER 631 (faculty for sale of two flagons on open market) and *Re St Gregory's, Tredington* [1972] Fam 236 (communion plate). See also *Re St Michael and All Angels, Great Torrington* cited in note 2 on p 100, below.

The same Measure (section 12) provides for a procedure by archdeacon's certificate in place of the issue of a faculty in certain cases. The procedure applies to any application received by the registrar of a diocese from the incumbent and churchwardens, and supported by a resolution of the parochial church council, for authority to carry out repairs to a church not involving any substantial change in the structure of the building nor affecting its appearance externally or internally, or repairs to the contents of a church not materially affecting their nature or appearance, or the redecoration of a church or its contents, or any alteration in the heating system not involving a substantial change in the appearance of the church externally or internally. Provided the application is supported by a certificate from the incumbent and churchwardens that notice of the intended application has been given (in the prescribed manner) in the parish, and that opportunity to object has been given to all persons having interest, the registrar will refer it to the archdeacon; and he can either issue a certificate, with the approval of the advisory committee provided for by the Measure, authorising the work, or direct that an application be made to the consistory court for a faculty. An archdeacon's certificate is sufficient authority for the work without a faculty. The chancellor may follow the same procedure in regard to any other application which he considers unlikely to give rise to any controversy or dissatisfaction in the parish, and not important enough to justify the expense of faculty proceedings. The advisory committee (the Diocesan Advisory Committee for the Care of Churches) can give advice to intending applicants for faculties, if they request it.[1]

1 See the Faculty Jurisdiction Rules 1967 (SI 1967/1002) and the Faculty Jurisdiction (Amendment) Rules 1987 (SI 1987/2266) as to application for archdeacon's certificate, petition for faculty and procedure generally, and forms.

If an addition to or alteration in the church is in fact made without a faculty and is therefore illegal, neither a churchwarden nor anyone else is entitled to do away with it, but a faculty for removal must be applied for.[1] On the other hand, application may be made for a confirmatory faculty authorising the continuance of the addition or alteration. On petition for a faculty for the removal of an ornament, a confirmatory faculty is often made the subject of a cross-petition.[2]

The court may order any person responsible for the execution of work, or the introduction or removal of articles, without the authority of a faculty, to pay the expenses of putting the matter right, and costs.[3]

The property in the goods and ornaments of the church is in the churchwardens, and they hold them on behalf of the parishioners. They must keep an inventory, and on going out of office hand over the goods and the inventory to their successors.[4] The churchwardens cannot, therefore, dispose of any of the church's property without the consent both of the parishioners, given now by the parochial church council, and of the Ordinary; but having such consent they may legally dispose of the property, provided both the churchwardens join in the disposal.[5]

1 *Ritchings v Cordingley* (1868) LR 3 A & E 113.
2 *Gardner v Ellis* (1874) LR 4 A & E 265. See *Re St Michael and All Angels, Great Torrington* [1985] 1 All ER 993 for a recent case involving a confirmatory faculty, which does not have retrospective effect (*Re St Mary's, Balham* [1978] 1 All ER 993).
3 Faculty Jurisdiction Measure 1964, s 5. And see *Re Woldingham Churchyard* [1957] 2 All ER 323, and *Re St Mary's, Balham* cited above.
4 Canon E1.
5 See Prideaux, pp 333–335; and *Re St Helen's, Brant Broughton* [1974] Fam 16, as to the onus of proof when a faculty is sought.

CHAPTER TEN

The Sittings in the Church and the Maintenance of Order

I. THE SITTINGS

It is a common law right of every parishioner to have a seat in the parish church, without payment, provided there is room for him.[1] Even if there is no seat available, a parishioner has still the right to enter the church in order to attend divine service.[2] The churchwardens have the right of allocating the seats in the church amongst the parishioners, and also of giving them to non-parishioners, so long as this does not interfere with the rights of parishioners to have seats.[3] In exercising this power they act as the deputies of the Ordinary, and they are bound to obey any directions given by him. It is the duty of the churchwardens to allot the seats in the church to those parishioners requiring the same, and a parishioner to whom a seat has been allotted is entitled to occupy that seat at every ordinary service held in the church, whether on Sunday or on a weekday. The churchwardens must not allow any other person to sit in an allotted seat until after the commencement of the service, and either a churchwarden or a stranger who interferes with the right of a person to sit in the seat allotted to him is liable to an

---

1 *Walter v Gunner and Drury* (1798) 1 Hag Con 314.
2 *Taylor v Timson* (1888) 20 QBD 671. See also p 54, above.
3 *Reynolds v Monkton* (1841) 2 Mood & R 384; and Canon F7.

action at common law.[1] The Ecclesiastical Jurisdiction Measure 1963 (section 82) has, however, abolished the old action in the ecclesiastical courts for perturbation of seat. If a person has enjoyed a certain seat for a considerable time, the churchwardens must not deprive him of it without giving him notice of their intention and an opportunity of making a protest and explanation.[2] In addition to their power of allotting the seats, and in exercise of their functions of ensuring the decent ordering of divine service, the churchwardens may direct in which of the unallotted seats the several members of the congregation who have not seats allotted to them shall sit.

Although every parishioner has a right to a seat in the church without payment, there seems no reason why the churchwardens should not, in making a distribution of the seats, accept a voluntary payment from those members of the congregation ready to pay for an allotted seat.[3]

It has been stated that the right to allocate seats in the chancel rests with the rector, whether clerical or lay, or even the vicar. But it is probable, though the matter is not free from doubt, that the right of the churchwardens, acting on behalf of the Ordinary, to arrange the sittings extends in general to seats in the chancel as well as to those in the body of the church.[4] Apart from this, neither

1 *Claverley (Vicar) v Parishioners* [1909] P 195.
2 *Horsfall v Holland* (1859) 6 Jur NS 278. See *Re St Mary's, Banbury* [1985] 2 All ER 611 as to the nature of the right to a pew, which is, strictly, an enclosure.
3 *St Saviour, Westgate-on-Sea (Vicar of) v St Saviour, Westgate-on-Sea Parishioners* [1898] P 217.
4 Prideaux (p 294) and Cripps (p 213) both pronounce in favour of the view stated in the text. See also *Clifford v Wicks* (1818) 1 B & Ald 498, per BAYLEY J, at p 506. Canon F7, laying down the right of the churchwardens to allocate the seats, goes on 'saving the right of the minister to allocate seats in the chancel'; and thus appears to be based on a view of the law opposite to that stated above.

the incumbent nor the parochial church council have any authority in the matter of the sittings; but the church-wardens should give due weight to their opinions. The above rules have certain exceptions, however, the chief of which are as follows:

(1) The rector of a church, whether lay or ecclesiastical, and sometimes the vicar, may be entitled by prescription to a particular pew or seat; and this may extend to his family.[1]

(2) There may be in the church an aisle or chapel which is the property of a private person, and in this case the churchwardens have no authority over the sittings in it.[2]

(3) There may be vested in a parishioner a perpetual right to occupy a certain pew, when this right will be good not only against the churchwardens but against the Ordinary also. This right may exist either by virtue of a faculty, or by prescription at common law, as a right appurtenant to the occupation of a dwelling-house (which, according to the better opinion, must be within the parish).[3]

If an aisle, chapel, or pew is vested in a private person as above described, the liability for repair is on the owner, and not on the churchwardens or council.

(4) Churches built under the Church Building Acts 1818 to 1884, and the New Parishes Act 1843 to 1884, are subject to any express provision as to sittings made under the Acts. In a church erected under the Church Building Act 1818, for example, two pews near the pulpit were to be set aside for the permanent use of

---

1 *Stileman-Gibbard v Wilkinson* [1897] 1 QB 749.
2 *Chapman v Jones* (1869) LR 4 Exch 273. And see p 90, above.
3 *Stocks v Booth* (1786) 1 Term Rep 428; *Philipps v Halliday* [1891] AC 228.

the minister, his family, and servants, not less than one-fifth of the seats (known as 'free seats') set apart for the use of the poor of the parish without payment, and the remainder let at rates to be fixed by the Ecclesiastical Commissioners (now the Church Commissioners).

The Church Building and New Parishes Acts were largely repealed by the New Parishes Measure 1943. This repeal does not alter the rules obtaining under the Acts in regard to the sittings in the churches built under them;[1] but the Measure of 1943 does not contain any similar provisions about the sittings in the churches built under it, and the general and ancient rules previously stated appear to govern the sittings in these.

2. THE MAINTENANCE OF ORDER

To the churchwardens belongs the duty of maintaining order in the church and churchyard, particularly during the performance of divine service. 'The duty of maintaining order and decorum in the church lies immediately upon the churchwardens, and if they are not present, or being present do not repress any indecency, they desert their proper duty.'[2] Canon F15 requires the churchwardens and their assistants not to suffer the church 'to be profaned by any meeting therein for temporal objects inconsistent with the sanctity of the place, nor the bells to be rung at any time contrary to the direction of the minister'; and not to suffer any person to behave in the

1 S 32 (1) of the New Parishes Measure 1943 expressly preserved any existing right to charge rents for sittings in churches built under the repealed Acts.
2 Sir Wm Scott (as he then was) in *Cox v Goodday* (1811) 2 Hag Con 138. Canon B20, however, imposes on the minister the general duty to 'banish all irreverence' in the practice and performance of the music.

church, porch, or churchyard during the time of service so as to create disturbance. They are to take care that nothing is done therein contrary to the law of the church or the realm; and if any person is guilty of riotous, violent or indecent behaviour, whether in time of divine service or not, or of disturbing, vexing, troubling, or misusing any minister officiating, they are to restrain the offender and if necessary proceed against him according to law. A good deal of this repeats the provisions of the Ecclesiastical Courts Jurisdiction Act 1860, referred to at the end of this chapter.

During the performance of divine service it is, therefore, the duty of the churchwardens to preserve quiet in the church and churchyard, to see that no-one behaves improperly, even though he is making no noise (for example, they may remove the hat of a man who refuses to take it off[1]), and to see that nothing interrupts the minister and others taking part in the service. In order to preserve order they may use an amount of force necessary for the occasion. Thus they may remove from the church a person who continues to disturb the service, and may even remove a person before the commencement of the service, if he shows an intention to make a disturbance.[2] This being the case, there seems no reason why a churchwarden should not prevent persons from entering the church at all, if they come with the intention of disturbing the service.[3] In the case of *Haw v Planner* (1666)[4] the court said that the churchwardens might 'switch boys playing in the churchyard, or any disturbers of the peace in time of divine service'; but STEPHEN J, in *Taylor v Timson*[5] said

1 *Haw v Planner* (1666) 2 Keb 124.
2 *Burton v Henson* (1842) 10 M & W 105.
3 See *Worth v Terrington* (1845) 13 M & W 781.
4 2 Keb 124.
5 (1888) 20 QBD 671 at 679.

'I do not recommend anyone to act on the whipping part
of the case.' If a person behaves improperly in a church
at a time other than that of divine service, or is a trespasser,
it seems that here again the churchwardens have authority
to remove him.[1]

It must be remembered, however, that the manner of
the administration of divine service is entirely within the
discretion of the minister, and the churchwardens have
no power to interfere with his conduct of the service. If
the minister conducts the service in an irregular manner,
they, or the parochial church council, should make representations to the bishop. It is, in short, the duty of the
churchwardens to maintain order for the administration
of the service by the minister. If the minister himself is
'guilty of any act grossly offensive', the churchwardens
and even private persons may interpose to preserve the
decorum of public worship; but that would be 'a case
of instant and overbearing necessity that supersedes all
ordinary rules'.[2]

Under the Ecclesiastical Courts Jurisdiction Act 1860
it is an offence to be guilty of 'riotous, violent, or indecent
behaviour' in a church (or churchyard) whether during
divine service or not; and to 'molest, disturb, vex, or
trouble' a clergyman conducting divine service. It is indecent behaviour within this statute to interrupt a service
by shouting and similar conduct;[3] and 'divine service'
includes a service of holy communion although
accompanied by various illegal practices.[4] A churchwarden (or constable) may arrest any person making a

1 See *Jarratt v Steele* (1820) 3 Phillium 167, and *Worth v Terrington*,
   above.
2 Sir Wm SCOTT (as he then was) in *Hutchins v Denziloe and Loveland*
   (1792) 1 Hag Con 170.
3 *Abrahams v Cavey* [1968] 1 QB 479.
4 *Matthews v King* [1934] 1 KB 505.

disturbance, and take him before a court of summary jurisdiction.[1]

Although it is the duty of the churchwardens to preserve order during divine service, they are not the only persons who have authority to do so. It was decided in *Glever v Hynde*[2] that at common law any person present at divine service might remove anyone making a disturbance there, by the same rule of law that allows a man to abate a nuisance; and in *Cox v Goodday*,[3] Lord STOWELL said that occasion might arise when the minister himself would be justified in interposing to preserve order, but he should do so with caution, and only in a case of necessity.

Canon F16 provides that if a church or chapel is to be used 'for a play, concert, or exhibition of films or pictures, the minister shall take care that the words, music and pictures are such as befit the House of God, are consonant with sound doctrine, and make for the edifying of the people'; and requires the minister first to consult the local authorities as to fire precautions and the like. Under the Theatres Act 1968 a licence to perform a play must be obtained from the licensing authority.

---

1 This Act abolished the former jurisdiction of the ecclesiastical courts
   to try cases of brawling, unless committed by a clergyman.
2 (1673) 1 Mod Rep 168.
3 (1811) 2 Hag Con 138.

CHAPTER ELEVEN

The Churchyard and other Consecrated Burial Places

The freehold of the churchyard annexed to the parish church is in the rector, or if there is no rector, in the vicar.[1] If there is a lay rector, the vicar has the possession of the churchyard for ecclesiastical purposes.[2] The rector (or, if there is none, the vicar) may exercise rights of property over the churchyard.[3] He may, for example, take for his use the grass growing there; and he may bring an action in the high court in respect of his freehold for trespass to the churchyard. The felling of trees is regulated by section 20 of the Repair of Benefice Buildings Measure 1972. They may be cut down only with the consent of the parsonages board established under the Measure,[4] unless they are so dangerous as to require felling immediately.

The rights of the freeholder over the churchyard are subject to the important qualification that it is consecrated ground set apart for the burial of the parishioners, and he must do nothing which would interfere with their rights, nor must he in any way desecrate the churchyard. He may

1 If the right of presentation has been suspended, the freehold is in the bishop.
2 *Greenslade v Darby* (1868) LR 3 QB 421,
3 And dispose of unconsecrated churchyard which is not needed, with the authority of the consistory court (*Re St Mary Magdalene, Paddington* [1980] 1 All ER 279).
4 See p 28, above.

not, for example, turn cattle in which trample on the graves or injure the tombstones; but the grazing of sheep may be permitted. In a proper case the parochial church council may obtain an injunction.[1]

All parishioners, and certain non-parishioners, have the right to be buried in the churchyard.[2]

To the parochial church council now belongs the duty of maintaining the churchyard in decent order and repair,[3] and the rules already given[4] with regard to the liability to repair the fabric of the church are generally applicable to the case of the churchyard. In addition to keeping the churchyard in order generally, the council must see that it is properly fenced and that the fences are maintained in good repair; and unless in a particular case the liability falls on someone else—an adjoining landowner, for example, may by custom be liable to repair a fence—the cost will fall on the council.[5] A power to contribute to the expense of maintaining a churchyard or other burial place is conferred on burial authorities by the Local Government Act 1972.[6]

The council would also seem to have inherited from

1 *Marriott v Tarpley* (1838) 9 Sim 279; *Batten v Gedye* (1889) 41 Ch D 507. It was formerly the duty of the churchwardens to proceed in these matters, but their functions in this respect devolved on the council (Parochial Church Councils (Powers) Measure 1956, s 4 (1) (ii)); see Halsbury, Vol 14, para 581. Guidance generally, and forms of agreement on various matters may be found in *The Churchyards Handbook* (Church House Publishing, Great Smith Street, London SW1).

2 See p 73, above for a full statement of the rights of burial.

3 Parochial Church Councils (Powers) Measure 1956, s 4 (1) (ii) (*c*).

4 See p 91.

5 See Canons F13 and F14.

6 S 214. The burial authorities are the councils of districts, London boroughs, parishes and communities, the Common Council of the City of London, and the parish meetings of parishes having no parish council.

the churchwardens the duty of making and maintaining footpaths across the churchyard, in order to afford the parishioners access to the church and to the various parts of the churchyard. The making of a new footpath requires a faculty.[1]

Failure to keep the churchyard, and the paths and tombstones in it, and even the church itself, in a proper state of repair may result in injury to persons using or visiting the churchyard, giving rise to a claim against the council or others responsible. The Occupiers' Liability Acts 1957 to 1984 are in point. Liability may of course be covered by insurance.

It is the duty of the council, not the churchwardens, to protect generally the rights of the parishioners in the churchyard. If, for instance, a dispute as to the boundary of the churchyard arises with a neighbouring landowner, or there is a question of the existence of a right of way to the church or churchyard, the council may, and in a proper case should, bring an action in the high court to determine the matter.[2] Under the old law, proceedings for trespass or injury to the church or churchyard were brought in the ecclesiastical courts. But it seems that, since the Ecclesiastical Jurisdiction Measure 1963, they must now be brought in the ordinary courts, at any rate if the person sued is a layman.[3]

It is the duty of the churchwardens to maintain order in the churchyard, both during the performance of divine service and at other times, and to see that it is not used

---

1 *Walter v Mountague* (1836) 1 Curt 253. As to a license to make occasional use of a churchyard (eg for escape in case of fire) see *Re St Mary Aldermary* [1985] 2 All ER 445.

2 See *St Edmundsbury and Ipswich Diocesan Board of Finance v Clark (No 2)* [1973] 3 All ER 902.

3 *Quilter v Newton* (1690) Carth 151. See note 1 on p 109, above; and p 128, below.

for secular purposes, but preserved for the sacred uses for which it has been set apart.[1]

As in the case of the church itself, so in the case of the churchyard, if it is desired to make any alteration in the condition of the churchyard or make any addition thereto, it is, in general, necessary to obtain a faculty.[2] The burial of the dead may of course take place without a faculty, and the incumbent may sanction the erection in the churchyard of tombstones and monuments of an ordinary character.[3] His consent to such erection should always be sought, but his right of veto should be exercised with discretion and is subject to the control of the Ordinary.[4] It is his duty to protect the churchyard by refusing to allow the erection of monuments of improper size or shape or having thereon improper inscriptions; and if it is desired to erect a monument of an extraordinary kind a faculty must be obtained.[5] When a monument or tombstone is erected in a churchyard, the property therein is

1 See p 104, above.
2 See *Morley Borough Council v St Mary the Virgin, Woodkirk* [1969] 3 All ER 952, and *Re St Peter's, Bushey Heath* [1971] 2 All ER 704, for the grant of a faculty for secular user. See also p 97, note 2, above; and *The Churchyards Handbook* (p 109, note 1, above), particularly pp 56–62, 97–110.
3 *Maidman v Malpas* (1794) 1 Hag Con 205.
4 *Keet v Smith* (1876) 1 PD 73. And in *Re Little Gaddesden Churchyard* [1933] P 150, the incumbent, who had refused to sanction a memorial of white marble, was overruled and a faculty granted. In many dioceses directions have been issued as to the material and dimensions of monuments. See also *Re St Peter, Kineton* [1967] 1 WLR 347.
5 See *Bardin v Calcott* (1789) 1 Hag Con 14. Two more recent cases are *Re Woldingham Churchyard* [1957] 2 All ER 323 (confirmatory faculty granted for a cross on a boulder, but refused for kerbs and chips); and *Re St Mary The Virgin, Ilmington* [1962] P 147 (faculty allowing an inscription asking for prayers for the dead). See pp 96–100, above.

in those who erected the same, and they, or the relatives of the deceased, may repair it. The parochial church council may, in default, do the work, and probably ought to do so if the tomb is in a dangerous state. A faculty may be granted for moving, demolishing, altering or doing any other work to a monument, even without the consent of the owner.[1] A faculty should be applied for if it is desired to reorganise the churchyard by, for example, removing or laying flat a number of headstones; and the Diocesan Advisory Committee for the Care of Churches may first be asked for its advice. If anyone injures a tombstone, the owner has a right of action against him.[2]

When an existing churchyard or burial ground was enlarged, or an additional burial ground provided under the Church Building Acts (the Act of 1819 in particular), the freehold of the new ground was vested in the person in whom the freehold of the ancient churchyard was vested—usually the incumbent of the parish church. Land bought for a burial ground under the New Parishes Measure 1943, which repealed most of the earlier Acts, vests in the incumbent.[3] The above rules relating to the care of the churchyard and other matters are applicable generally to these burial grounds.

Burial authorities have power under the Local Government Act 1972 to provide and maintain cemeteries, and they may apply to the bishop of the diocese to consecrate

1 Faculty Jurisdiction Measure 1964, s 3. The power extends to monuments in the church as well. As to the grant of a faculty for the disinterment of remains, see *Norfolk County Council v Knights* [1958] 1 All ER 394 and *Re Matheson* [1958] 1 All ER 202.

2 See *Spooner v Brewster* (1825) 3 Bing 136. And see an article in the Law Journal of 22 September 1950 (Vol 100), at p 524, as to various ways of making valid provision for the upkeep of a tomb.

3 S 6 (1) of the Church Property (Miscellaneous Provisions) Measure 1960.

any part of the ground. The incumbent of any parish within the area chargeable with the expenses of the cemetery is then under an obligation to perform funeral services in the consecrated part, to the same extent as in the churchyard.[1]

Regarding churchyards closed for burials, the Local Government Act 1972 imposes on parochial church councils the obligation to maintain them, by keeping them in decent order and the walls and fences in good repair. But a council may free itself of this liability by serving a written request on the parish or community council, or other appropriate body, to take over the maintenance.[2] Control over a closed churchyard does not however pass to the local authority, and it remains in the incumbent, to be exercised in accordance with the principles previously stated.[3]

1 See on these matters Local Government Act 1972, s 214 and Sch 26; Local Authorities' Cemeteries Order 1977 (SI 1977/204), in particular art 17. And see chapter 6, p 75, above, and note 6 on p 109, above.
2 Local Government Act 1972, s 215.
3 See *Re St Clement, Eastcheap* [1964] P 20, for a faculty case giving parishioners rights over a disused churchyard. And see s 30 of the Pastoral Measure 1983 for pastoral schemes relating to churchyards and burial grounds.

CHAPTER TWELVE

Churches not Parochial and Chapels of Ease

Many parishes have within their boundaries, besides parish churches (of which there may be more than one[1]), other churches or chapels constituting places of public worship for the parishioners. Some of these churches or chapels have districts assigned to them, others not. The Church Building Acts 1818 to 1884, and the New Parishes Acts 1843 to 1884, used to provide for the creation of ecclesiastical districts as well as parishes. But section 86 of the Pastoral Measure 1968 converted all districts constituted for ecclesiastical purposes by or under any Act or Measure, and all other ecclesiastical districts with a minister having a separate cure of souls, including any district belonging or annexed to any church or chapel, into parishes with full parochial status. The church, or chapel, has become the parish church.

The only exception to this is the conventional district, that is, a district carved out of one or more parishes by agreement between the bishop and the incumbent or incumbents. The district is placed under a curate-in-charge. The parishioners remain parishioners of their original parish and retain their rights to attend public worship in the parish church and to the performance of the other services there, unless, as regards marriage, the place of worship of the conventional district has been

1 See s 27 of the Pastoral Measure 1983.

114

licensed for marriages under section 20 of the Marriage Act 1949.

But for the purposes of the Church Representation Rules 'parish' is defined, in rule 44, to include a conventional district, and 'minister' to include a curate licensed to the charge of the district. Accordingly a conventional district should have its separate electoral roll, annual church meeting, and parochial church council, in accordance with these Rules.[1] The church of the district will also possess its own churchwardens.[2]

Churches or chapels which are neither parish churches, nor the churches of conventional districts, are known as chapels of ease. Many of these are of ancient foundation. To quote an old work:

> 'Chapels of ease; some of them have parochial rights to christen and bury, and are therefore called parochial chapels by way of distinction, from others that have no such privilege; and these differ in nothing from churches, but in the want of rectories and indowments, the mother being to be served before the daughter.
>
> Those chapels of ease which are not parochial, cannot bury or christen; but are only used for the ease of the parishioners to hear the word of God read and preached, and to join in prayers.'[3]

Chapels of ease came into existence also under the nineteenth-century Acts above mentioned, the Union of Benefices Measures 1923 to 1952 (repealed), and the New Parishes Measure 1943; and they may arise by virtue of a pastoral scheme under Part II of the Pastoral

1 See chapter 4.
2 See the definitions in section 13 of the Churchwardens (Appointment and Resignation) Measure 1964.
3 Degge, *Parson's Counsellor*, p 227.

Measure 1983, replacing the Pastoral Measure 1968. Under section 29 of the 1983 Measure the bishop is to provide for public worship in a parish which has no church or chapel by licensing a building for the purpose. He may also designate such a licensed building, or any church (or chapel) not a parish church, as a parish centre of worship, when it will be deemed to be a parish church.[1]

In any parish where there are two or more churches or buildings licensed for public worship the annual church meeting may make a scheme under rule 16 of the Church Representation Rules to provide for the election to the parochial church council of representatives of the laity in a manner which will ensure due representation of the congregation of each church or building, or for the election of a district church council for a district served by the church or building, or for both these purposes. The district church council may have functions of the parochial church council delegated to it. Similarly, deputy church-wardens may be appointed for any such church or building.

The incumbent of a parish, having the cure of souls throughout his parish, will himself officiate in a chapel of ease there, or he may appoint a curate to do so; in either case he is entitled to the fees and offerings.[2] His consent must be obtained to another clergyman officiating in the chapel, and he has general authority to determine all matters relating thereto which are in his province.

If there is no scheme for deputy wardens as above, the churchwardens of the parish church will, as a general rule, be the wardens of a chapel of ease in the parish. There

---

1 A building so designated is not subject to the faculty jurisdiction, unless this is directed by the bishop under s 6 of the Faculty Jurisdiction Measure 1964.
2 See Burn, *Ecclesiastical Law*, Vol 1, pp 300, 305.

may, however, be a long-standing custom to elect separate wardens for a district served by a chapel of ease.

The law set out in the former part of this book with regard to the powers and duties of the incumbent, church-wardens and council in relation to the parish church is generally applicable to a chapel of ease within the parish. The repair of a chapel of ease was formerly provided for by rates levied on the landholders within the chapelry,[1] but the parochial church council will now raise the money required as it thinks fit, and not necessarily only from the persons attending the chapel. The council has general control over the financial affairs of the parish; and, therefore, including money collected at the offertory, it has power jointly with the incumbent to dispose of all moneys collected in the chapel of ease, and may decide all questions relating to the expenses of the chapel.[2]

1 See Burn, Vol 1, p 304.
2 'Church' when used in any Measure, eg The Inspection of Churches Measure 1955 (see p 92, above), includes a consecrated chapel unless the contrary intention appears: see the Interpretation Measure 1925. Canons F1 to 18 apply to chapels as to churches.

CHAPTER THIRTEEN

Ecclesiastical Courts, and their Jurisdiction

The history of the ecclesiastical courts in this country has, since the sixteenth century, been a story of gradual loss of jurisdiction.[1] This jurisdiction has chiefly been lost in one of the three following ways:

(1) It has been lost by transfer to the temporal courts. An outstanding example of this is the transfer in 1858 of divorce and matrimonial causes to a court for divorce and matrimonial causes, and of testamentary matters to a court of probate,[2] both of which courts were replaced by the High Court of Justice.[3] A more recent example of transfer of jurisdiction is afforded by the Chancel Repairs Act 1932, which has been mentioned in chapter 9. Many statutes have provided for the punishment in the criminal courts of offences which were formerly punishable only in the ecclesiastical courts, as, for example, bigamy, and incest.[4] The jurisdiction of

1 For a short and clear account of the history of the jurisdiction of the Ecclesiastical Courts, see Holdsworth, *History of English Law*, Vol 1, Chap VII.
2 Matrimonial Causes Act 1857, and Court of Probate Act 1857.
3 The Probate Divorce and Admiralty Division of the High Court was renamed the Family Division by s 1 of the Administration of Justice Act 1970 (now s 5 of the Supreme Court Act 1981).
4 1 Jac 1, c 11, Offences against the Person Act 1861, s 57 (bigamy); Sexual Offences Act 1956, ss 10 and 11 (incest). Note also the Ecclesiastical Courts Jurisdiction Act 1860, p 106, above.

the ecclesiastical courts has thus, by implication, been taken away.[1]

(2) It has been abolished by statute, as, for example, by the Compulsory Church Rate Abolition Act 1868; and by the Ecclesiastical Courts Jurisdiction Act 1860, which ended the jurisdiction of the ecclesiastical courts relating to offences of brawling committed by laymen.[2]

(3) The jurisdiction, although not taken away by law, became obsolete, owing to a changed moral or social attitude. In the sixteenth century the ecclesiastical courts exercised a wide jurisdiction over clergy and laity alike, in respect of offences against morals—'for the good of their souls'. Examples of such offences were adultery, drunkenness, usury, neglect to attend church, and many others. Much of this jurisdiction was, expressly or by implication, taken away by statute. As for the rest, it was said by Lord PENZANCE in *Phillimore v Machon*:[3] 'It cannot, I think, be doubted that a recurrence to the punishment of the laity for the good of their souls by ecclesiastical courts would not be in harmony with modern ideas, or the position which ecclesiastical authority now occupies in the country.' The learned judge evidently disapproved of the attempt to revive 'a jurisdiction which, if it has not expired, has so long slumbered in peace'. A belated attempt to assert that this jurisdiction over the laity still remained, made in the high court case of *Blunt v Park Lane Hotel Ltd*,[4] met with no greater success.

---

1 *Phillimore v Machon* (1876) 1 PD 481.
2 See p 87, note 1, and p 107, note 1, above.
3 Above, at pp 487, 489.
4 [1942] 2 KB 253.

The coup de grâce was delivered by the Ecclesiastical Jurisdiction Measure 1963. The ecclesiastical courts and their jurisdiction had long been recognised to be in need of reform; and that reform was effected by the Measure of 1963. The courts were reconstructed, their procedure revised, the older Acts and Measures relating to the discipline of the clergy repealed and replaced,[1] and certain outmoded jurisdiction of the courts abolished. The Ecclesiastical Judges and Legal Officers Measure 1976 has fixed retiring ages for judges of ecclesiastical courts and provided for the office of registrar of a province and of a diocese.

The consistory court of each diocese (in the diocese of Canterbury called the 'commissary court') remains the basic court of the system. It is the court of the bishop, presided over by the chancellor of the diocese (known as the 'commissary general' in the diocese of Canterbury), who is appointed by the bishop.[2]

The principal matters in respect of which jurisdiction is exercised by the consistory court are the following:

(a) charges against clergymen in respect of offences other than those involving matters of doctrine, ritual or ceremonial;

(b) faculty suits;

(c) disputes about rights of patronage;

(d) proceedings for penalties under certain provisions of the Pluralities Act 1838;[3]

(e) any other proceedings which lay in the consistory court before the new Measure was passed, not

1 Thus the Church Discipline Act 1840, the Public Worship Regulation Act 1874, and the Clergy Discipline Act 1892 were all repealed.
2 Ecclesiastical Jurisdiction Measure 1963, ss 1 (1) and 2. Under proposed legislation the Lord Chancellor's approval will be required.
3 Eg for failing to reside on the benefice: see p 25, above.

being proceedings in respect of which jurisdiction has been expressly abolished by the Measure.[1]

More will be said later about the jurisdiction of the consistory courts. Above these courts comes the court of the archbishop of the province, which hears appeals from them. In the province of Canterbury the court is called the Arches Court of Canterbury, and in the province of York the Chancery Court of York. Each court is composed of five judges. There is a single chief judge of both courts, appointed by the two archbishops jointly, with Her Majesty's approval. In respect of his jurisdiction in the province of Canterbury he is styled the Dean of the Arches, and in respect of his jurisdiction in the province of York he is styled the Auditor: in the Measure he is referred to as the Dean of the Arches and Auditor. Of the other judges of each provincial court, two are in holy orders, appointed by the prolocutor of the Lower House of Convocation, and two are laymen possessing judicial experience, appointed by the chairman of the House of Laity, after consulting the Lord Chancellor.[2]

The Arches Court of Canterbury and the Chancery Court of York hear appeals from the consistory courts, within their respective provinces, in cases (a), (b), (d) and (e) above: that is to say, where a clergyman is charged with an offence not involving doctrine, ritual or ceremonial; faculty cases; proceedings under the Pluralities Act; and the other proceedings saved by case (e). But, in faculty suits, the appeal is to the archbishop's court only if no matter involving doctrine, ritual or ceremonial is involved.[3] A further and final appeal in this class of faculty

1 Measure of 1963, s 6.
2 Measure of 1963, ss 1 (2) and 3.
3 For these and other appeals except those in case (a) the court is composed of the Dean of the Arches and Auditor alone (ibid, s 47). The appeal court may substitute its own discretion for that of the

suit lies to the Judicial Committee of the Privy Council.[1]
This is the only instance in which the jurisdiction of the
Judicial Committee in ecclesiastical causes was preserved
by the Measure.[2]

The Measure of 1963 set up a new court, the Court of
Ecclesiastical Causes Reserved, principally for hearing
matters which do involve doctrine, ritual or ceremonial.
The court consists of five judges appointed by Her
Majesty, two being persons who hold or have held high
judicial office, and the other three being persons who are
or have been diocesan bishops.[3] The lay members of
the court, like all lay judges of ecclesiastical courts, are
required by the Measure to be communicants. This court
has both original and appellate jurisdiction. It tries any
charge against a clergyman for an offence against ecclesiastical law which involves a matter of doctrine, ritual or
ceremonial; and any suit of *duplex querela,* ie when a
clergyman presented to a living complains that the bishop
will not admit him. It has also, in its appellate capacity,
jurisdiction to hear appeals from the consistory courts
in faculty cases involving matter of doctrine, ritual or
ceremonial.[4] The findings of the Court of Ecclesiastical
Causes Reserved may themselves be reviewed, on petition
to Her Majesty, by a Commission of Review appointed
by Her, consisting of three Lords of Appeal and two
lords spiritual of Parliament.[5] In a matter of doctrine, the

---

chancellor (*Re St Gregory's, Tredington* [1971] 3 All ER 269).
　　See the Ecclesiastical Jurisdiction (Faculty Appeals) Rules 1965
(SI 1965/251) for the procedure for all appeals in faculty cases.
1　Ss 7 and 8.
2　It has jurisdiction in respect of pastoral schemes: see note 2, p 22,
　above.
3　S 5.
4　S 10. The chancellor of the diocese will certify whether the case
　involves doctrine, ritual or ceremonial.
5　S 11.

Commission is to have the assistance of five advisers, bishops or other theologians.[1]

Parties appear in the ecclesiastical courts either personally or by proctors, and solicitors now act as proctors.[2] Either a barrister or a solicitor may argue a cause in an ecclesiastical court.[3] Legal aid will be available.[4]

To return now to the jurisdiction of the courts, and first that of the consistory courts. These courts, as already stated, will hear any charge against a clergyman for an 'offence under the Measure'. This means any offence (not involving matter of doctrine, ritual or ceremonial) against ecclesiastical law committed by a priest or deacon, including conduct unbecoming to the office and work of a clerk in holy orders, or serious, persistent or continuous neglect of duty.[5] Proceedings for unbecoming conduct cannot be taken in respect of political opinions or activities, or for neglect of duty in respect of political opinions. But they will still lie in respect of offences involving immorality, for example; or in respect of illegalities with regard to the fabric of the church, or the performance of the church services (where no question of doctrine, ritual or cer-

1 S 48.
2 Solicitors Act 1974, s 19.
3 Halsbury, Vol 14, para 1298.
4 Church of England (Legal Aid and Miscellaneous Provisions) Measure 1988, ss 1–4; Church of England (Legal Aid) Rules 1988 (SI 1988/1175).
5 S 14. In *Bland v Archdeacon of Cheltenham* [1972] Fam 157, the Arches Court of Canterbury held that the offence of refusing to baptise a child did not involve matters of doctrine, ritual or ceremonial, although the reason for the refusal might be partly based on doctrinal views; and therefore the offence was triable by the consistory court. The clergyman had in fact been charged, for this and other acts, with serious neglect of duty, and the court said that acts or omissions constituting ecclesiastical offences should be charged as such rather than as serious neglect of duty or conduct unbecoming.

emonial is involved); or for publicly performing services in a parish without the consent of the incumbent.[1]

Proceedings for any offence of the kind described in the preceding paragraph may be instituted against an incumbent, stipendiary curate or curate in charge of a conventional district by six or more persons on the electoral roll of the parish or district; or by the incumbent against a stipendiary curate; or (against any priest or deacon) by any person authorised by the bishop. They are begun by the laying of a written complaint, in a prescribed form, before the registrar of the diocese.[2] The bishop will interview in private both the accused clergyman and the complainant or complainants; and he may then either decide that nothing further is to be done in the matter, or refer the complaint for inquiry by an examiner, who will be selected from a panel of barristers or solicitors drawn up by the diocesan synod.[3] The examiner, after an inquiry before which each party may lay evidence on affidavit, and be represented by an adviser, or assisted by a friend, decides whether there is a case for the accused to answer.[4] If there is, the bishop will nominate a fit person to promote a complaint in the consistory court. The case is then tried by the chancellor sitting with four assessors, two priests and two laymen, who act as a jury.[5]

---

1 *Nesbitt v Wallace* [1901] P 354. The performance of services in a private house without such consent may be permissible; see p 53, note 5, above. As to the housebound or detained, see p 69, above.
2 Ecclesiastical Jurisdiction Measure 1963, ss 18 and 19.
3 Ibid, ss 23 and 30 and Second Schedule, Part I.
4 S 24.
5 Ss 25, 28 and 30, and Second Schedule, Part II. Under s 31 the bishop may at any time, with the consent of the accused, himself deal with the matter, and pronounce censure. See the Ecclesiastical Jurisdiction (Discipline) Rules 1964 (SI 1964/1755) for the procedure for the trial of offences under the Measure.

Of the other jurisdiction exercised by the consistory courts, the faculty jurisdiction has already been explained.[1] It constitutes, in practice, by far the largest part of their jurisdiction. It is permissive only; that is, the court can authorise the doing of an act, and it may also order the removal of something illegally placed in a consecrated place, and generally order the setting right of what has been done wrong. But it has no power to make a mandatory order, as, for instance, an order directing the manner in which a war memorial, which has been moved into an unsuitable position in a church, should be dealt with after removal.[2] Nor can the faculty jurisdiction be exercised punitively.[3]

If an offence involving matter of doctrine, ritual or ceremonial is alleged against a clergyman, the initial procedure is the same as that outlined above in respect of other offences. But the bishop, unless he decides that the matter should be carried no further, will refer the complaint for inquiry by a committee consisting of one member of the Upper House of Convocation, two members of the Lower House, and two diocesan chancellors; and the committee will decide (a majority will be enough) whether there is a case to answer. If there is, the accused will be tried by the new court, the Court of Ecclesiastical Causes Reserved; except that, if the committee consider that the offence was too trivial to warrant further proceedings, or that it was committed under extenuating circumstances, or that further proceedings would not be in the interest of the Church of England, they may dismiss the complaint, reporting their action to Convocation.[4] If the case is to be tried, the Upper House

1 See p 96, above.
2 *Re St John-in-Bedwardine, Worcester* [1961] 3 All ER 216.
3 *Re St Mary, Tyne Dock (No 2)* [1958] P 156.
4 Ecclesiastical Jurisdiction Measure 1963, s 42.

of Convocation nominates a fit person to promote a complaint before the court.[1] The Court of Ecclesiastical Causes Reserved is to sit with not less than three nor more than five advisers, who are to be eminent theologians or liturgiologists. The court is not to be bound by any decision of the Judicial Committee of the Privy Council in relation to matters of doctrine, ritual or ceremonial.[2]

If a clergyman is found guilty of the offence with which he is charged, whether by the consistory court, or by the Court of Ecclesiastical Causes Reserved for an offence concerning doctrine, ritual or ceremonial, the court will pronounce censure, that is, spiritual punishment, upon him.[3] The censures that can be pronounced are, in ascending order of gravity: rebuke (newly introduced by the Measure); monition, which is an order to do or refrain from doing a specified act; suspension, which is disqualification, for a specified time, from exercising any right or performing any duty in connection with the preferment held, or from residing in or within a specified distance of the house of residence; inhibition, which is disqualification, for a specified time, from exercising any of the functions of a clergyman; deprivation, which is removal from preferment and disqualification from holding any future preferment.[4] Where, however the offence is one involving matter of doctrine, ritual or ceremonial, a rebuke or monition only may follow unless

1 Ecclesiastical Jurisdiction Measure 1963, s 43.

2 S 45.

3 Ss 28 and 45.

4 S 49 (1). See *Bland*, cited in note 5 on p 123, above, for a statement of the considerations which should govern the pronouncement of sentence, particularly of deprivation.

   The intention of the Measure was apparently to abolish excommunication, which had long been obsolete; though all it does expressly is to abolish 'imprisonment in consequence of being excommunicated' (s 82 (4)).

the accused has already been admonished in respect of an offence of the same, or substantially the same, nature.[1]

In case of suspension, the clergyman cannot be readmitted to his benefice, or, in a case of inhibition, he cannot again exercise the functions of a clergyman, unless he satisfies the bishop of his good conduct during the term of his suspension or inhibition. In a case of deprivation the sentence will not extend to any preferment to which the bishop, with the consent of the archbishop, may appoint him; and the archbishop may direct that the deprivation is to cease altogether.[2]

Where a censure of deprivation has been pronounced, the bishop may depose the clergyman from holy orders, but only after serving on him a notice of his intention, and the clergyman may appeal within one month to the archbishop.[3] If after deprivation or deposition a clergyman receives a free pardon from the Crown, he will be restored to his former position, including any preferment he previously held, if it has not meanwhile been filled.[4]

A clergyman who is disqualified by reason of any censure from performing any function in the Church, and nevertheless performs it, is guilty of an offence under the Measure.[5]

Deprivation may also follow if a clergyman has been convicted in the secular courts of a criminal offence and sentenced to imprisonment, or if a decree of divorce or judicial separation has been pronounced against him on certain grounds, and in other instances named in the Measure. The bishop refers the case to the archbishop,

1 S 49 (3).
2 S 49 (2) and (5).
3 S 50.
4 S 53.
5 S 54.

with his recommendation, and any representations the clergyman may have made to him in writing.[1]

No criminal proceedings can henceforward be taken against anyone in an ecclesiastical court except in accordance with the Measure of 1963; and the proceedings which can be so taken are limited to proceedings against the clergy of the nature already described in this chapter (excluding those against bishops and archbishops, which do not fall within the ambit of this book)[2] It follows therefore that a criminal suit, such as previously lay against the churchwardens for wrongly interfering with the churchyard, or with the ordering of the services,[3] or against an organist for disobeying the directions of the minister as to when the organ is to be played,[4] or even against a lay person not holding any office, if he does something which it is illegal to do without a faculty,[5] will no longer be possible. The Measure indeed expressly abolishes the jurisdiction of the consistory courts to hear and determine proceedings against lay officers of a church, and also by way of suit for perturbation of seat.[6] It is odd that the Measure stopped short at expressly abolishing criminal jurisdiction over the laity in general, but this undoubtedly is its effect. Other means of enforcing the law must be sought: for example, an action for trespass where appropriate; or a petition for a faculty for removal

---

1 S 55, as amended by the Ecclesiastical Jurisdiction (Amendment) Measure 1974.
2 S 69.
3 *Walter v Mountague* (1836) 1 Curt 253; *Hutchins v Denziloe and Loveland* (1792) 1 Hag Con 170.
4 *Wyndham v Cole* (1875) 1 PD 130.
5 *Bardin v Calcott* (1789) 1 Hag Con 14; *Adlam v Colthurst* (1867) LR 2 A & E 30.
6 S 82 (2).

of something placed in a church without authority, when the person responsible may be ordered to pay expenses and costs.[1]

1 See p 100, above.

Church of England Assembly (Powers) Act 1919

1. **Definitions**—In this Act—

    (1) 'The National Assembly of the Church of England' (hereinafter called 'the Church Assembly') means the Assembly constituted in accordance with the Constitution set forth in the Appendix to the Addresses presented to His Majesty by the Convocations of Canterbury and York on the tenth day of May nineteen hundred and nineteen and laid before both Houses of Parliament;

    (2) 'The Constitution' means the Constitution of the Church Assembly set forth in the Appendix to the Addresses presented by the Convocations of Canterbury and York to His Majesty as aforesaid;

    (3) 'The Legislative Committee' means the Legislative Committee of the Church Assembly appointed in accordance with the provisions of the Constitution;

    (4) 'The Ecclesiastical Committee' means the Committee established as provided in section two of this Act;

    (5) 'Measure' means a legislative measure intended to receive the Royal Assent and to have effect as an Act of Parliament in accordance with the provisions of this Act.

2. **Establishment of an Ecclesiastical Committee.**—(1) There shall be a Committee of members of both Houses of Parliament styled 'The Ecclesiastical Committee'.

    (2) The Ecclesiastical committee shall consist of fifteen members of the House of Lords nominated by the Lord Chan-

cellor, and fifteen members of the House of Commons nominated by the Speaker of the House of Commons, to be appointed on the passing of this Act to serve for the duration of the present Parliament and thereafter to be appointed at the commencement of each Parliament to serve for the duration of that Parliament.

Any casual vacancy occurring by the reason of the death, resignation, or incapacity of a member of the Ecclesiastical Committee shall be filled by the nomination of a member by the Lord Chancellor or the Speaker of the House of Commons, as the case may be.

(3) The powers and duties of the Ecclesiastical Committee may be exercised and discharged by any twelve members thereof, and the Committee shall be entitled to sit and to transact business whether Parliament be sitting or not, and notwithstanding a vacancy in the membership of the Committee. Subject to the provisions of this Act, the Ecclesiastical Committee may regulate its own procedure.

3. Measures passed by Church Assembly to be submitted to Ecclesiastical Committee.—(1) Every measure passed by the Church Assembly shall be submitted by the Legislative Committee to the Ecclesiastical Committee, together with such comments and explanations as the Legislative Committee may deem it expedient or be directed by the Church Assembly to add.

(2) The Ecclesiastical Committee shall thereupon consider the measure so submitted to it, and may, at any time during such consideration, either of its own motion or at the request of the Legislative Committee, invite the Legislative Committee to a conference to discuss the provisions thereof, and thereupon a conference of the two committees shall be held accordingly.

(3) After considering the measure, the Ecclesiastical Committee shall draft a report thereon to Parliament stating the nature and legal effect of the measure and its views as to the expediency thereof, especially with relation to the consitutional rights of all His Majesty's subjects.

(4) The Ecclesiastical Committee shall communicate its

report in draft to the Legislative Committee, but shall not present it to Parliament until the Legislative Committee signify its desire that it should be so presented.

(5) At any time before the presentation of the report to Parliament the Legislative Committee may, either on its own motion or by direction of the Church Assembly, withdraw a measure from further consideration by the Ecclesiastical Committee; but the Legislative Committee shall have no power to vary a measure of the Church Assembly either before or after conference with the Ecclesiastical Committee.

(6) A measure may relate to any matter concerning the Church of England, and may extend to the amendment or repeal in whole or in part of any Act of Parliament, including this Act:

Provided that a measure shall not make any alteration in the composition or powers or duties of the Ecclesiastical Committee, or in the procedure in Parliament described by section four of this Act.

(7) No proceedings of the Church Assembly in relation to a measure shall be invalidated by any vacancy in the membership of the Church Assembly or by any defect in the qualification or election of any member thereof.

4. Procedure on measures reported on by the Ecclesiastical Committee.—When the Ecclesiastical Committee shall have reported to Parliament on any measure submitted by the Legislative Committee, the report, together with the text of such measure, shall be laid before both Houses of Parliament forthwith, if Parliament be then sitting, or, if not, then immediately after the next meeting of Parliament, and thereupon on a resolution being passed by each House of Parliament directing that such measure in the form laid before Parliament should be presented to His Majesty, such measure shall be presented to His Majesty, and shall have the force and effect of an Act of Parliament on the Royal Assent being signified thereto in the same manner as to Acts of Parliament:

Provided that if, upon a measure being laid before Parliament, the Chairman of Committees of the House of Lords and the Chairman of Ways and Means in the House of Commons acting in consultation shall be of opinion that the measure deals with two or more different subjects which might be more properly divided, they may, by joint agreement, divide the measure into two or more separate measures accordingly, and thereupon this section shall have effect as if each of the measures resulting from such division had been laid before Parliament as a separate measure.

5. Short title.—This Act may be cited as the Church of England Assembly (Powers) Act 1919.

APPENDIX 2

Church Representation Rules[1]

1 As published by Church House Publishing, incorporating amendments to 1 January 1985.

APPENDIX I

Synodical Government Forms

APPENDIX I I

General Provisions relating to Parochial Church Councils

PART I CHURCH ELECTORAL ROLL

FORMATION OF ROLL

1. (1) There shall be a church electoral roll (in these rules referred to as 'the roll') in every parish, on which the names of lay persons shall be entered as hereinafter provided. The roll shall be available for inspection by bona fide inquirers.

(2) A lay person shall be entitled to have his name entered on the roll of a parish, if he—

(*a*) is baptised;
(*b*) is a member of the Church of England or of a Church in communion with the Church of England;
(*c*) is of sixteen years or upwards;
(*d*) is resident in the parish, or, if not so resident, has habitually attended public worship in the parish during a period of six months prior to enrolment; and
(*e*) has signed the form of application for enrolment set out in section 1 of Appendix I to these rules.

Provided that where a lay person will have his sixteenth birthday after the intended revision of the electoral roll or the preparation of a new roll but on or before the date of the annual parochial church meeting, he may complete a form of application for enrolment and his name shall be enrolled but with effect from the date of his birthday.

(3) A person shall be entitled to have his name on the roll of each of any number of parishes if he is entitled by virtue of paragraph (2) of this rule to have his name entered on each roll;

but a person whose name is entered on the roll of each of two or more parishes must choose one of those parishes for the purpose of the provisions of these rules which prescribe the qualifications for election to a deanery synod, a diocesan synod or the General Synod or for membership of a parochial church council under rule 12 (1) (*e*) or of a deanery synod under rule 19 (3) (*b*).

(4) The roll shall, until a parochial church council has been constituted in a parish, be formed and revised by the minister and churchwardens (if any), and shall, after such council has been constituted, be kept and revised by or under the direction of the council. Reference in this rule to a parochial church council shall, so far as may be necessary for giving effect to these rules, be construed as including references to the minister and churchwardens (if any).

(4A) Where a new parish is created by a pastoral scheme, the roll of that parish shall in the first instance consist—

(*a*) in the case of a parish created by the union of two or more former parishes, of the rolls of those parishes combined to form one roll;

(*b*) in any other case, of the names of the persons whose names are at the date of the coming into existence of the new parish entered on the roll of a parish the whole or any part of which forms part of the new parish and who are either resident in the new parish or have habitually attended public worship therein.

(5) The parochial church council shall appoint a church electoral roll officer to act under its direction for the purpose of carrying out its functions with regard to the electoral roll.

(6) The names of persons who are entitled to have their names entered upon the roll of the parish shall, subject to the provisions of these rules, be from time to time added to the roll. No name shall be added to or removed from the roll except by the authority of the parochial church council and it shall be the duty of that council to keep the roll constantly up to date

and to cause names to be added and removed as from time to time required by these rules.

(7) Subject to the provision of this rule, a person's name shall, as the occasion arises, be removed from the roll, if he—

(*a*) has died; or

(*b*) becomes a clerk in Holy Orders; or

(*c*) signifies in writing his desire that his name should be removed; or

(*d*) ceases to reside in the parish, unless after so ceasing he continues, in any period of six months, to attend public worship in the parish, unless prevented from doing so by illness or other sufficient cause; or

(*e*) is not resident in the parish and has not attended public worship in the parish during the preceding six months, not having been prevented from doing so by illness or other sufficient cause; or

(*f*) was not entitled to have his name entered on the roll at the time when it was entered.

(8) The removal of a person's name from the roll under any of the provisions of these rules shall be without prejudice to his right to have his name entered again, if he has or acquires that right.

(9) The roll shall where practicable contain a record of the address of every person whose name is entered on the roll, but a failure to comply with this requirement shall not prejudice the validity of any entry on the roll.

REVISION OF ROLL AND PREPARATION OF NEW ROLL

2. (1) Except in a year in which a new roll is prepared, the roll of a parish shall be revised annually by or under the direction of the council. Notice of the intended revision in the form set out in section 2 of Appendix I to these rules shall be affixed by the minister or under his direction on or near the principal door of every church in the parish and every building in the parish licensed for public worship and remain so affixed for a period of not less than fourteen days before the commencement of the revision. The revision shall be completed not less that fifteen days or more than twenty-eight days before the annual parochial church meeting.

(2) Upon every revision all enrolments or removals from the roll which have been effected since the date of the last revision (or since the formation of the roll, if there has been no previous revision) shall be reviewed, and such further enrolments or removals from the rolls as may be required shall be effected.

(3) After the completion of the revision, a copy of the roll as revised shall, together with a list of the names removed from the roll since the last revision (or since the formation of the roll, if there has been no previous revision), be published by being exhibited continuously for not less than fourteen days before the annual parochial church meeting on or near the principal door of the parish church in such manner as the council shall appoint. Subject to the proviso to rule 1 (2), no name shall be entered upon or removed from the roll during the period in any year between the completion of the revision and the close of the annual parochial church meeting.

(4) Not less than two months before the annual parochial church meeting in the year 1990 and every succeeding sixth year notice in the form set out in section 3 of Appendix I to these rules shall be affixed by the minister or under his direction on or near the principal door of every church in the parish and every building in the parish licensed for public worship and remain so affixed for a period of not less than fourteen days. On the affixing of the notice a new roll shall be prepared.

At every service held on each of the two Sundays within the period of fourteen days beginning with the date of the affixing of the notice or, in the case of a church in which no service is held on either of those Sundays, at every service held in that church on the first Sunday after that date the person conducting the service shall inform the congregation of the preparation of the new roll.

(5) The parochial church council shall take reasonable steps

to inform every person whose name is entered on the previous roll that a new roll is being prepared and that if he wishes to have his name entered on the new roll he must apply for enrolment. No such steps need be taken with respect to any person whose name could be removed from the previous roll under rule 1 (7).

(6) The new roll shall be prepared by entering upon it the names of persons entitled to entry under rule 1 (2), and fresh application shall be required from persons whose names were entered on the previous roll. A person whose name was so entered shall not be disqualified for entry on the new roll by reason only of his failure to comply with the conditions specified in rule 1 (2) (*d*), if he was prevented from doing so by illness or other sufficient cause, and the circumstances shall be stated on the application form. The preparation of the new roll shall be completed not less than fifteen days or more than twenty-eight days before the annual parochial church meeting.

(7) After the completion of the new roll, a copy shall be published by being exhibited continuously for not less than fourteen days before the annual parochial church meeting on or near the principal door of the parish church in such manner as the council shall appoint. No name shall be entered upon or removed from the roll during the period in any year between the completion of the new roll and the close of the annual parochial church meeting. On the publication of the new roll the previous roll shall cease to have effect.

(8) Upon the alteration of the boundaries of any parishes the parochial church council of the parish from which any area is transferred shall enquire from the persons resident in that area whose names are entered on the roll of the parish, whether they wish to have their names transferred to the roll of the other parish. The parochial church council shall remove the names of persons answering in the affirmative from its own roll and shall inform the parochial church council of the parish in which such persons now reside, which shall enter the names on its roll without any application for enrolment being required.

PROCEDURAL PROVISIONS RELATING TO ENTRY AND REMOVAL OF
NAMES

3. (1) When a person applying for enrolment on the roll of any
parish signifies his desire that his name should be removed from
the roll of any other parish, notice of that fact shall be sent by
the parochial church council receiving the application to the
parochial church council of that other parish.

(2) When the name of any person is removed from the roll
of the parish owing to his having become resident in another
parish, notice of that fact shall, whenever possible, be sent by
the parochial church council of the first mentioned parish to
the parochial church council of the last mentioned parish.

CERTIFICATION OF NUMBERS ON ROLLS

4. (1) Not later than the 1st June—

(*a*) in any year immediately preceding a year in which elections of members of deanery synods or diocesan synods will
fall due,
(*b*) in any year being the fourth year after the last preceding
election of members of the House of Laity of the General
Synod,

the numbers of names on the roll of each parish shall be certified
to the secretary of the diocesan synod and the secretary of
the deanery synod, and the certificate shall be signed by the
chairman, vice-chairman, secretary or church electoral roll
officer of the parochial church council:

Provided that, if the General Synod is at any time dissolved
before the fourth year after the last preceding election of the
House of Laity or before this rule has taken effect during that
year, the General Synod or the Presidents thereof may give
directions requiring the number of names on the roll of each
parish to be certified as aforesaid within such time as may be
specified and the directions may, if the dissolution is known to
be impending, be given before it occurs.

(2) A copy of such certificate shall be affixed at or near to the

principal door of every church in the parish and every building licensed for public worship in the parish when the certificate is sent to the secretary of the diocesan synod, and shall remain so affixed for a period of not less than fourteen days.

(3) Any question as to the accuracy of any certificate given under this rule shall be decided in such manner as the diocesan synod or the bishop's council and standing committee shall determine.

PROVISION WITH RESPECT TO PERSON WHOSE NAME IS ON GUILD CHURCH ROLL

4A. (1) A person whose name is entered on the roll of a guild church shall for the purpose of the provisions of these rules which prescribe the qualifications for election to a deanery synod, a diocesan synod or the House of Laity of the General Synod, or for membership of a deanery synod under rule 19 (3) (*b*), be deemed to be a person whose name is on the roll of the parish in which the guild church is, and references in those provisions or in rule 1 (3) to a person whose name is on the roll of a parish or on the roll of each of two or more parishes, and in rule 37 to entry on the roll of a parish, shall be construed accordingly.

(2) In this rule 'guild church' means a church in the City of London designated and established as a guild church under the City of London (Guild Churches) Acts 1952 and 1960.

PART II PAROCHIAL CHURCH MEETINGS AND COUNCILS

ANNUAL MEETINGS

5. (1) In every parish there shall be held not later than the 30th April in each year the annual parochial church meeting (hereafter in these rules referred to as 'the annual meeting').

(2) All lay persons whose names are entered on the roll of the parish shall be entitled to attend the annual meeting and to

take part in its proceedings, and no other lay person shall be so entitled.

(3) A clerk in Holy Orders shall be entitled to attend the annual meeting of the parish and take part in its proceedings—

(*a*) if he is either beneficed in or licensed to the parish or any other parish in the area of the benefice to which the parish belongs; or

(*b*) if he is resident in the parish and is not beneficed in or licensed to any other parish; or

(*c*) if he is not resident in the parish and is not beneficed or licensed to any other parish, the parochial church council with the concurrence of the minister has declared him to be an habitual worshipper in the parish, such declaration being effective until the conclusion of the annual meeting in the year in which a new roll is prepared under rule 2 or his ceasing to be an habitual worshipper in the parish whichever is the earlier, but without prejudice to a renewal of such declaration; or

(*d*) if he is a co-opted member of the parochial church council in accordance with rule 12 (1) (*g*).

(4) Without prejudice to paragraphs (2) and (3) of this rule—

(*a*) all the members of the team of a team ministry shall be entitled to attend, and take part in the proceedings of, the annual meeting of the parish or each of the parishes in the area of the benefice for which the team ministry is established, and where the area of a group ministry includes the area of a benefice for which a team ministry is established, all the vicars in that ministry shall be entitled to attend, and take part in the proceedings of, the annual meeting of each of the other parishes in the area for which the group ministry is established;

(*b*) all the incumbents and priests in charge in a group ministry shall be entitled to attend, and take part in the proceedings of, the annual meeting of each of the parishes in the area for which the group ministry is established.

(5) Where two or more benefices are held in plurality and a

team ministry is, or is to be, established for the area of one of those benefices, then, if a pastoral scheme provides for extending the operation of the team ministry, so long as the plurality continues, to the area of any other benefice so held, paragraph (4) of this rule shall have effect as if the references to the area of the benefice were references to the combined area of the benefices concerned.

CONVENING OF MEETING

6. (1) The annual meeting shall be convened by the minister of the parish by a notice in the form set out in section 4 of Appendix I to these rules affixed on or near to the principal door of every church in the parish, and every building licensed for public worship in the parish, for a period including the last two Sundays before the day of the meeting.

(2) The annual meeting shall be held at such place on such date and at such hour as shall be directed by the previous annual meeting, or by the parochial church council (which may vary any direction given by a previous annual meeting) or in the absence of any such direction as shall be appointed by the minister.

(3) During the vacancy of the benefice or curacy or when the minister is absent or incapacitated by illness or any other cause, the vice-chairman of the parochial church council, or if there is no vice-chairman, or if he is unable or unwilling to act, the secretary of or some other person appointed by that council shall have all the powers vested in the minister under this rule.

(4) The annual meeting shall be held at a place within the parish unless the parochial church council decide otherwise.

(5) The minister of a new parish created by a pastoral scheme, or, in the absence of the minister, a person appointed by the bishop, shall as soon as possible after the scheme comes into operation convene a special parochial church meeting, and, subject to paragraph (6) of this rule, the provisions of these rules relating to the convening and conduct of the annual

meeting shall apply to a special meeting convened under this paragraph.

(6) A special meeting so convened and held in the month of November or the month of December may, if the meeting so resolves, be for all purposes under these rules the annual meeting for the succeeding year, and a special meeting so convened shall in any event be for all such purposes the annual meeting for the year in which it is so convened and held.

CHAIRMAN

7. (1) The minister, if present, or, if he is not present, the vice-chairman of the parochial church council, or, subject to paragraph (2) of this rule, if he also is not present, a chairman chosen by the annual meeting shall preside thereat.

(2) Where a parish is in the area of a benefice for which a team ministry is established, and a vicar in that ministry is entitled to preside at an annual meeting of that parish by virtue of a provision in a pastoral scheme or the bishop's licence assigning to the vicar the duties, or a share in the duties, of the chairmanship of the annual meeting of that parish, then, if both he and the vice-chairman of the parochial church council are not present at that meeting, but the rector in that ministry is present, the rector shall preside thereat.

(3) In the case of an equal division of votes, the chairman of the meeting shall have a second or casting vote, unless it is a case where rule 10 (8) applies; but no clerical chairman shall have a vote in the election of the parochial representatives of the laity.

BUSINESS

8. (1) The annual meeting shall receive from the parochial church council and shall be free to discuss—

(*a*) a copy or copies of the roll;

(*b*) an annual report on the proceedings of the parochial church council;

(*c*) an annual report on the financial affairs of the parish;

(*d*) the audited accounts of the parochial church council for the year ending on the 31st December immediately preceding the meeting;

(*e*) an audited statement of the funds and property, if any, remaining in the hands of the parochial church council at the said date;

(*f*) a report upon the fabric, goods and ornaments of the church or churches of the parish; and

(*g*) a report on the proceedings of the deanery synod.

(2) The council shall cause a copy of the said audited accounts and the said audited statement to be affixed on or near the principal door of every church in the parish and every building licensed for public worship in the parish at least seven days before the annual meeting.

(3) Such accounts and statement shall be submitted to the annual meeting for approval. If approved, they shall be signed by the chairman of the meeting, who shall then deliver them to the parochial church council for publication, and the parochial church council shall forthwith cause them to be published and affixed for a period of at least fourteen days on or near the principal door of every church in the parish and every building licensed for public worship in the parish and at such other conspicuous place or places in the parish as the parochial church council think appropriate and shall cause a copy to be sent to the secretary of the diocesan board of finance.

(4) The annual meeting shall in the manner provided by rule 10 of these rules—

(*a*) elect in every third year parochial representatives of the laity to the deanery synod;

(*b*) elect parochial representatives of the laity to the parochial church council;

(*c*) elect sidesmen;

and the elections shall be carried out in the above order.

(5) The annual meeting shall appoint the auditors to the council.

(6) Without prejudice to the foregoing provisions and rule 6 (6), a special parochial church meeting convened under rule 6 (5) shall, in addition to other business—

(*a*) decide on the number of members of the parochial church council who are to be the elected representatives of the laity;
(*b*) elect in the manner provided by rule 10 parochial representatives of the laity to the deanery synod, if such representatives are required to be elected in the year for which that meeting is the annual meeting by virtue of rule 6 (6).

(7) Any person entitled to attend the annual meeting may ask any question about parochial church matters, or bring about a discussion of any matter of parochial or general church interest, by moving a general resolution or by moving to give any particular recommendation to the council in relation to its duties.

(8) The annual meeting shall have power to adjourn and to determine its own rules of procedure.

(9) The secretary of the parochial church council (or another person appointed by the meeting in his place) shall act as a clerk of the annual meeting, and shall record the minutes thereof.

QUALIFICATIONS OF PERSONS TO BE CHOSEN OR ELECTED BY ANNUAL MEETINGS

9. (1) Subject to the provisions of rule 1 (3), the qualifications of a person to be elected a parochial representative of the laity to either of the bodies referred to in the last preceding rule are that—

(*a*) his name is entered on the roll of the parish; and
(*b*) he is an actual communicant member of the Church of England or, in the case of election to the parochial church

council, an actual communicant member of any Church in communion with the Church of England; and

(*c*) in the case of election to the parochial church council, he is of seventeen years or upwards, and in the case of election to the deanery synod, he is of eighteen years or upwards:

Provided that the registrar of the diocese shall not be qualified for election to any of the said bodies in that diocese.

(1A) Notwithstanding paragraph (1) hereof, a baptised person who—

(*a*) is of communicant status in another Church which sub-scribes to the doctrine of the Holy Trinity; and

(*b*) is in good standing in that Church; and

(*c*) is an habitual worshipper and a communicant at the parish church or at some other building licensed for public worship in the parish; and

(*d*) is of seventeen years and upwards,

may, with the prior permission of the bishop, be nominated for election as a parochial representative of the laity to the parochial church council:

Provided that at least two-thirds of the parochial rep-resentatives of the laity to the parochial church council shall have the qualifications set out in paragraph (1) hereof.

(2) The qualification of a person to be elected a sidesman is that his name is entered on the roll of the parish.

(3) No person shall be elected under the last preceding rule unless he has signified his consent to serve or there is in the opinion of the meeting sufficient evidence of his willingness to serve.

CONDUCT OF ELECTIONS AT ANNUAL MEETINGS

10. (1) Subject to the provisions of any scheme made under rule 10A and for the time being in force, this rule shall apply to all elections at annual meetings.

(2) All candidates for election at an annual meeting must be nominated and seconded by persons entitled to attend the annual meeting, and in the case of parochial representatives of the laity, by persons whose names are entered on the roll of the parish. A candidate shall be nominated or seconded either before the meeting in writing or at the meeting.

(3) If the number of candidates nominated is not greater than the number of seats to be filled, the candidates nominated shall forthwith be declared elected.

(4) If more candidates are nominated than there are seats to be filled, the election shall take place at the annual meeting.

(5) No clerk in Holy Orders shall be entitled to vote in the election of any parochial representatives of the laity.

(6) Each person entitled to vote shall have as many votes as there are seats to be filled but may not give more than one vote to any one candidate.

(7) Votes may be given—

(*a*) on voting papers, which must be signed by the voter on the reverse thereof; or
(*b*) if no person present objects thereto, by show of hands.

(8) Where owing to an equality of votes an election is not decided the decision between the persons for whom the equal numbers of votes have been cast shall be taken by lot.

(9) The result of any election by an annual meeting shall be announced as soon as practicable by the person presiding over the election, and a notice of the result shall in every case be affixed on or near the principal door of every church in the parish and every building licensed for public worship in the parish, and shall bear the date on which the result is declared. The notice shall remain affixed for not less than fourteen days.

(10) Returns of parochial representatives of the laity elected to the deanery synod shall be sent to the secretary of that synod.

Variation of method of election by scheme

10A. (1) The annual meeting may make a scheme which provides that the election of parochial representatives of the laity
to the parochial church council or to the deanery synod or to
both that council and that synod shall be conducted by the
method of the single transferable vote under rules, with the
necessary modifications, made by the General Synod under rule
33 (4) and for the time being in force.

(2) No scheme under this rule shall be valid unless approved
by at least two-thirds of the persons present and voting at the
annual meeting nor shall it be operative until the next ensuing
annual meeting. Every such scheme shall, on its approval, be
communicated to the bishop's council and standing committee
of the diocesan synod which shall consider the scheme, determine whether or not the scheme shall come into operation and
inform the secretary of the parochial church council of its
decision.

CONDUCT OF ELECTIONS OF CHURCHWARDENS

11. (1) If elections of churchwardens take place at meetings of
parishioners under section 3 of the Churchwardens (Appointment and Resignation) Measure 1964 either because there has
been no joint consent under section 2 of that Measure or because
there is no minister, the elections shall be conducted, announced
and notified in the same manner as elections under rule 10,
except that all persons entitled to attend the meeting of parishioners other than the minister shall be entitled to nominate
and vote at such elections of churchwardens.

(2) The Churchwardens (Appointment and Resignation)
Measure 1964 shall be amended as follows—

(*a*) in section 2 (1) for the words 'not later in the year
than during the week following Easter week' there shall be
substituted the words 'not later than the 30th April in each
year';
(*b*) sections 4, 5, 6 and 11 (3) shall be repealed; and

(*c*) section 3 (6) shall not apply to elections of churchwardens.

PAROCHIAL CHURCH COUNCIL

Members

12. (1) Subject to the provisions of rule 1 (3), the parochial church council shall consist of—

(*a*) all clerks in Holy Orders beneficed in or licensed to the parish;

(*b*) any deaconess or lay worker licensed to the parish;

(*bb*) in the case of a parish in the area of a benefice for which a team ministry is established, all the members of the team of that ministry;

(*c*) the churchwardens, being actual communicant members of the Church of England whose names are on the roll of the parish;

(*d*) such, if any, of the readers whose names are on the roll of the parish, as the annual meeting may determine;

(*e*) all persons whose names are on the roll of the parish and who are lay members of any deanery synod, diocesan synod or the General Synod;

(*f*) such number of representatives of the laity as the annual meeting may decide, and so that the number determined may be altered from time to time by a resolution passed at any annual meeting, but such resolution shall not take effect before the next ensuing annual meeting; and

(*g*) co-opted members, if the parochial church council so decides, not exceeding in number one-fifth of the representatives of the laity elected under the last preceding sub-paragraph of this paragraph, and being either clerks in Holy Orders or actual lay communicant members of the Church of England of seventeen years of age or upwards. The term of office of a co-opted member shall be until the conclusion of the next annual meeting; but without prejudice to his being co-opted on subsequent occasions for a similar term, subject to and in accordance with the provisions of these rules.

(1A) Any person chosen, appointed or elected as a church-warden of a parish, being an actual communicant member of the Church of England whose name is on the roll of the parish, shall as from the date on which the choice, appointment or election, as the case may be, is made be a member of the parochial church council of the parish by virtue of this para-graph until he is admitted to the office of churchwarden, and he shall thereafter continue to be a member of that council by virtue of sub-paragraph (*c*) of paragraph (1) of this rule unless and until he ceases to be qualified for membership by virtue of that sub-paragraph.

(2) If—
(*a*) the name of any person, being an elected representative of the laity, is removed from the roll of the parish under rule 1, or
(*b*) any such person refuses or fails to apply for enrolment when a new roll for the parish is being prepared,

that person shall cease to be a member of the parochial church council of the parish on the date on which his name is removed from the roll or, as the case may be, on the date on which the new roll is completed, but the preceding provisions are without prejudice to any right which that council may have to make that person a co-opted member.

(3) Where a group ministry is established the incumbents of all benefices in the group, every priest in charge of any benefices therein and where the area of the group ministry includes the area of a benefice for which a team ministry is established, all the vicars in that ministry shall be entitled to attend meetings of the parochial church councils of all the parishes in the area for which the group ministry is established. They shall be entitled to receive documents circulated to members of councils of which they are not themselves members and to speak but not to vote at meetings of such councils.

(4) Where two or more benefices are held in plurality and a team ministry is, or is to be, established for the area of one of those benefices, then, if a pastoral scheme provides for extend-

ing the operation of the team ministry, so long as the plurality continues, to the area of any other benefice so held, paragraphs (1) (*bb*) and (3) of this rule shall have effect as if the references to the area of the benefice were references to the combined area of the benefices concerned.

General Provisions relating to Parochial Church Councils

13. The provisions in Appendix II to these rules shall have effect with respect to parochial church councils, and with respect to the officers, the meetings and the proceedings thereof:

Provided that a parochial church council may, with the consent of the diocesan synod, vary the said provisions, in their application to the council.

Term of Office

14. (1) Representatives of the laity on the parochial church council of a parish shall hold office from the conclusion of the annual meeting until the conclusion of the next annual meeting of the parish:

Provided that the annual meeting may decide that one-third only (or the number nearest to one-third) of the representatives of the laity elected to the council shall retire from office in every year. In any case where it is so decided, the representatives of the laity to retire from office at each annual meeting shall be those who have been longest in office since last elected, and as between representatives of the laity elected on the same day, those to retire shall (unless they otherwise agree among themselves) be selected by lot. A representative of the laity shall in any event retire at the conclusion of the third annual meeting after that at which he was elected.

(2) Persons who are members of a parochial church council by virtue of their election as lay members of a deanery synod shall hold office for a term beginning with the date of their election and ending with the 31st May next following the election of their successors.

Limitation on Years of Service

15. The annual meeting may decide that no representative of the laity on the parochial church council may hold office for more than a specified number of years continuously and may also decide that after a specified interval a person who has ceased to be eligible by reason of such decision may again stand for election as representative of the laity on the council.

Parishes with more than one Place of Worship

16. (1) In any parish where there are two or more churches or places of worship the annual meeting may make a scheme which makes provision for either or both of the following purposes, that is to say—

(*a*) for the election of representatives of the laity to the parochial church council in such manner as to ensure due representation of the congregation of each church or place; and

(*b*) for the election by the annual meeting for any district in the parish in which a church or place of worship is situated of a district church council for that district.

(2) A scheme for the election of any district church council or councils under the preceding paragraph shall provide for the election of representatives of the laity on to such council, for ex-officio members and for the chairmanship of such council and shall contain such other provisions as to membership and procedure as shall be considered appropriate by the annual meeting.

(3) Such a scheme may also provide for the delegation by the parochial church council to a district church council of such functions as it may specify and subject to the scheme the parochial church council may delegate to a district church council such of its functions as it shall think fit but not including (in either case) the functions of a parochial church council as interested parties under Part I of the Pastoral Measure 1983.

(4) A scheme may provide for the election or choice of one or two deputy churchwardens, and for the delgation to him or them of such functions of the churchwardens relating to any church or place as the scheme may specify, and the church-wardens may, subject to the scheme, delegate such of their said functions as they think fit to the deputy churchwarden or churchwardens.

(5) No scheme under this rule shall be valid unless approved by at least two-thirds of the persons present and voting at the annual meeting nor shall the scheme provide for it to come into operation until such date as the bishop's council and standing committee may determine being a date not later than the next ensuing annual meeting. Every such scheme shall on its approval be communicated to the bishop's council and standing committee of the diocesan synod which may determine—

(*a*) that the scheme shall come into operation; or
(*b*) that the scheme shall not come into operation; or
(*c*) that the scheme shall come into operation with specified amendments, if such amendments are approved by an annual or special parochial church meeting and the scheme as amended is approved by at least two-thirds of the persons present and voting at the meeting.

(6) Where a pastoral scheme establishing a team ministry, or an instrument of the bishop made by virtue of that scheme, makes, in relation to a parish in the area of the benefice for which the team ministry is established, any provision which may be made by a scheme under this rule, no scheme under this rule relating to that parish shall provide for the scheme to come into operation until on or after the date on which the provisions in question of the pastoral scheme or of the instrument, as the case may be, cease to have effect.

(7) A scheme under this rule may be varied or revoked by a subsequent scheme thereunder.

(8) Every member of the team of a team ministry shall have a right to attend the meetings of any district church council

elected for any district in a parish in the area of the benefice for which the team ministry is established.

(9) This rule shall be without prejudice to the appointment, in parishes with more than one parish church, of two church-wardens for each church under section 27 (5) of the Pastoral Measure 1983.

(10) In this rule 'place of worship' means a building or part of a building licensed for public worship.

Joint Parochial Church Councils and Group Councils

17. (1) Where there are two or more parishes within the area of a single benefice or two or more benefices are held in plurality, the annual meetings of all or some of the parishes in the benefice or benefices may make a joint scheme to provide—

(*a*) for establishing a joint parochial church council (hereinafter referred to as 'the joint council') comprising the ministers of the parishes and such numbers of representatives of each of those parishes elected by and from among the other members of the parochial church council of the parish as may be specified in the scheme;
(*b*) for the chairmanship, meetings and procedure of the joint council;
(*c*) for the delegation by the parochial church council of each such parish to the joint council of such of its functions, other than its functions as an interested party under Part I of the Pastoral Measure 1983, as may be so specified.

(2) Subject to the scheme and to any pastoral scheme or order made under paragraph 13 of Schedule 3 to the said Measure, the parochial church council of any such parish may delegate to the joint council such of its functions, other than its functions as an interested party under the said Part I, as it thinks fit.

(3) The joint council shall meet from time to time for the purpose of consulting together on matters of common concern.

(4) No scheme under this rule shall be valid unless approved by at least two-thirds of the persons present and voting at the annual meeting nor shall the scheme provide for it to come into operation until such date as the bishop's council and standing committee may determine being a date not later than the next ensuing annual meeting. Every such scheme shall on its approval be communicated to the bishop's council which may determine—

(*a*) that the scheme shall come into operation; or

(*b*) that the scheme shall not come into operation; or

(*c*) that the scheme shall come into operation with specified amendments, if such amendments are approved by an annual or special parochial church meeting and the scheme as amended is approved by at least two-thirds of the persons present and voting at that meeting.

(5) A special parochial church meeting of a parish to which this rule applies may be convened for the purpose of deciding whether to join in making such a scheme, and where such a meeting is convened the foregoing provisions shall have effect with the substitution for references to the annual meeting of references to the special meeting.

(6) Where a pastoral scheme or order, or any instrument of the bishop made by virtue of such a scheme or order, establishes a joint parochial church council for two or more of the parishes in a single benefice or two or more of the parishes in benefices held in plurality, no scheme under this rule relating to those parishes shall provide for the scheme to come into operation until on or after the date on which the provisions of the pastoral scheme, pastoral order or instrument, as the case may be, establishing the joint parochial church council cease to have effect.

(7) Where the provisions of a pastoral scheme or order for the holding of benefices in plurality are terminated under section 18 (2) of the Pastoral Measure 1983, any provision of a scheme under this rule establishing a joint parochial church council for all or some of the parishes of those benefices and the other

provisions thereof affecting that council shall cease to have effect on the date on which the first mentioned provisions cease to have effect.

(8) A scheme under this rule may be varied or revoked by a subsequent scheme thereunder.

Team Councils

17A. (1) Where a team ministry is established for the area of a benefice which comprises more than one parish the annual meetings of the parishes in that area may make a joint scheme to provide—

    (*a*) for establishing a team council comprising—
        (i) all the members of the team;
       (ii) every assistant curate, deaconess and lay worker licensed to any such parish; and
      (iii) such number of lay representatives elected by and from among the lay representatives of the parochial church council of each parish in the area as may be specified in the scheme;

(*b*) for the chairmanship, meetings and procedure of the team council; and

(*c*) for the delegation by the parochial church council of each such parish to the team council of such functions, other than its functions as an interested party under Part I of the Pastoral Measure 1983, as may be so specified.

(2) Subject to the scheme and to any pastoral scheme relating to the team council made under paragraph 4 (3) of Schedule 3 to the said Measure, the parochial church council of any such parish may delegate to the team council such of its functions, other than its functions as an interested party under the said Part I, as it thinks fit.

(3) The team council shall meet from time to time for the purpose of consulting together on matters of common concern.

(4) No scheme under this rule shall be valid unless approved

by at least two-thirds of the persons present and voting at the annual meeting nor shall the scheme provide for it to come into operation until such date as the bishop's council and standing committee may determine being a date not later than the next ensuing annual meeting. Every such scheme shall on its approval be communicated to the bishop's council and standing committee of the diocesan synod which may determine—

(*a*) that the scheme shall come into operation; or

(*b*) that the scheme shall not come into operation; or

`(*c*) that the scheme shall come into operation with specified amendments, if such amendments are approved by an annual or special parochial church meeting and the scheme as amended is approved by at least two-thirds of the persons present and voting at that meeting.

(5) A special parochial church meeting of a parish to which this rule applies may be convened for the purpose of deciding whether to join in making such a scheme, and where such a meeting is convened the foregoing provisions shall have effect with the substitution for references to the annual meeting of references to the special meeting.

(6) Where a pastoral scheme establishing a team ministry, or an instrument of the bishop made by virtue of that scheme, establishes a team council for that ministry, no scheme under this rule relating to that ministry shall provide for the scheme to come into operation until on or after the date on which the provisions of the pastoral scheme or of the instrument, as the case may be, establishing the team council cease to have effect.

(7) A scheme under this rule may be varied or revoked by a subsequent scheme thereunder.

Group Councils

17B. (1) Where a pastoral scheme establishes a group ministry, the annual meetings of the parishes in the area for which the group ministry is established may make a joint scheme to provide—

(*a*) for establishing a group council comprising—
> (i) all the members of the group ministry;
> (ii) every assistant curate, deaconess and lay worker licensed to any such parish; and
> (iii) such number of lay representatives elected by and from among the lay members of the parochial church council of each such parish as may be specified in the scheme;

(*b*) for the chairmanship, meetings and procedure of the group council; and

(*c*) for the delegation by the parochial church council of each such parish to the group council of such functions, other than its functions as an interested party under Part I of the Pastoral Measure 1983, as may be so specified.

(2) If the area of a group ministry includes the area of a benefice for which a team ministry is established, a scheme under this rule shall provide for the vicars in that ministry, as well as the rector, and all the other members of the team to be members of the group council.

(3) Paragraphs (2) to (7) of rule 17A shall apply in relation to a scheme under this rule as they apply in relation to a scheme under that rule with the modification that for the references to a team ministry and team council there shall be substituted references to a group ministry and a group council respectively.

SPECIAL AND EXTRAORDINARY MEETINGS

18. (1) In addition to the annual meeting the minister of a parish may convene a special parochial church meeting, and he shall do so on a written representation by not less than one-third of the lay members of the parochial church council; and the provisions of these rules relating to the convening and conduct of the annual meeting shall, with the necessary modifications, apply to a special parochial church meeting.

(2) On a written representation made to the archdeacon by not less than one-third of the lay members of the parochial

church council, or by one-tenth of the persons whose names are on the roll of the parish, and deemed by the archdeacon to have been made with sufficient cause, the archdeacon shall convene an extraordinary meeting of the parochial church council or an extraordinary parochial church meeting, and shall either take the chair himself or shall appoint a chairman to preside. The chairman, not being otherwise entitled to attend such meeting, shall not be entitled to vote upon any resolution before the meeting.

(3) In any case where the archdeacon is himself the minister, any representation under paragraph (2) of this rule shall be made to the bishop, and in any such case the references to the archdeacon in paragraph (2) of this rule shall be construed as references to the bishop, or to a person appointed by him to act on his behalf.

(4) All lay persons whose names are entered on the roll of the parish on the day which is twenty-one clear days before the date on which any special or extraordinary parochial church meeting is to be held shall be entitled to attend the meeting and to take part in its proceedings, and no other lay person shall be so entitled.

(5) A clerk in Holy Orders shall be entitled to attend any such meeting and to take part in its proceedings if by virtue of rule 5 (3), (4) or (5) he would have been entitled to attend the annual meeting of the parish had it been held on the same date, and no other such clerk shall be so entitled.

PART III DEANERY SYNODS

MEMBERSHIP

19. (1) A deanery synod shall consist of a house of clergy and a house of laity.

(2) The members of the house of clergy of a deanery synod shall consist of—

(*a*) the clerks in Holy Orders beneficed in or licensed to any parish in the deanery;

(*b*) any clerks in Holy Orders licensed to institutions in the deanery under the Extra-Parochial Ministry Measure 1967;

(*c*) any clerical members of the General Synod or diocesan synod resident in the deanery;

(*d*) such other clerks in Holy Orders holding the bishop's licence and resident or working in any part of the deanery as may be determined by or in accordance with a resolution of the diocesan synod;

(*e*) one retired clerk in Holy Orders who has attained the retiring age within the meaning of the Clergy Pensions Measure 1961 at the relevant date, chosen in such manner as may be approved by the bishop by and from among the retired clerks in Holy Orders who have attained that age at that date, are resident in the deanery and are not licensed to any parish in the deanery or to any institution therein under the said Measure of 1967.

(2A) Where an extra-parochial place is not in a deanery it shall be deemed for the purposes of these rules to belong to the deanery which it abuts and if there is any doubt in the matter a determination shall be made by the bishop's council and standing committee.

(2B) For the purposes of paragraph (2) (*e*) above the relevant date shall be the 31st December in the year immediately pre-ceding any election of the parochial representatives of the laity, and as soon as possible after that date the rural dean of the deanery shall inform the bishop of the number of clerks in Holy Orders who are qualified for membership of the deanery synod by virtue of that sub-paragraph.

(3) Subject to the provisions of rule 1 (3), the members of the house of laity of a deanery synod shall consist of the following persons, that is to say—

(*a*) the parochial representatives elected to the synod by the annual meetings of the parishes of the deanery;

(*b*) any lay members of the General Synod, a diocesan synod or an area synod constituted in accordance with section 17 of the Dioceses Measure 1978 whose names are entered on the roll of any parish in the deanery;

(*c*) if in the opinion of the bishop of the diocese any community of persons in the deanery who are in the spiritual care of a chaplain licensed by the bishop should be represented in that house, one lay person, being an actual communicant member of the Church of England of eighteen years or upwards, chosen in such manner as may be approved by the bishop by and from among the members of that community;

(*d*) such other lay persons, being deaconesses or lay workers licensed by the bishop to work in any part of the deanery, as may be determined by or in accordance with a resolution of the diocesan synod.

(4) The house of clergy and house of laity of a deanery synod may co-opt additional members of their respective houses, being clerks in Holy Orders or, as the case may be, lay persons who shall be actual communicant members of the Church of England of eighteen years or upwards:

Provided that the number of members co-opted by either house shall not exceed five per cent of the total number of members of that house or three, whichever is the greater.

ELECTION AND CHOICE OF MEMBERS

20. (1) The parochial representatives of the laity elected by annual meetings shall be so elected every three years, and shall hold office for a term of three years beginning with the 1st June next following their election.

(2) The numbers to be so elected from the several parishes shall be determined by resolution of the diocesan synod not later than the 31st December in the year preceding any such elections, and those numbers shall be related to the numbers of names on the rolls of the parishes as certified under rule 4 and provision may be made by the resolution for the separate representation of a district for which there is a district church council.

(3) Not later than the 31st December in the year preceding any such elections, the secretary of the diocesan synod shall certify to the secretary of each parochial church council the number of such representatives to be elected at the annual meeting of the parish and inform him of any provision for the separate representation of such a district as aforesaid and shall send to the secretary of each deanery synod copies of the certificates and information relating to the parishes of the deanery.

(4) Any person to be chosen as mentioned in rule 19 (2) (*e*) or 19 (3) (*c*) shall be so chosen every three years and shall hold office for a term of three years beginning with the 1st June next following the date on which he is so chosen.

(5) A resolution of the diocesan synod making provision under paragraph (2) (*d*) or (3) (*d*) of the last preceding rule for the membership of the clerks in Holy Orders or the deaconesses or lay workers therein mentioned may provide for the choice by a class of such persons of some of their number to be members, and for the term of office of persons so chosen.

(6) The diocesan synod shall exercise their powers under this and the last preceding rule so as to secure that the total number of members of any deanery synod in the diocese shall not be more than 150 and, so far as practicable, shall not be less than 50:

Provided that the maximum number of 150 may be exceeded for the purpose of securing that the house of laity is not less in number than the house of clergy.

For the avoidance of doubt it is hereby declared that the number 150 specified in this paragraph includes the maximum number of members who may be co-opted by each house.

VARIATION OF MEMBERSHIP OF DEANERY SYNODS BY SCHEME

21. (1) If it appears to the diocesan synod that the preceding rules in this Part relating to the membership of deanery synods ought to be varied to meet the special circumstances of the diocese or the deaneries and to secure better representation of clergy or laity or both on the deanery synods, they may make a scheme for such variation, and, if the scheme comes into operation under this rule, the said rules shall have effect subject to the scheme.

(2) Copies of every such scheme must be sent to members of the diocesan synod at least fourteen days before the session at which they are considered, and every such scheme shall require the assent of the house of bishops and of a two-thirds majority of the members of each of the other houses of the synod present and voting.

(3) A scheme approved by the diocesan synod as aforesaid shall be laid before the General Synod.

(4) If a member of the General Synod gives notice in accordance with the Standing Orders of that Synod that he wishes such a scheme to be debated, the scheme shall not come into operation unless it is approved by the General Synod.

(5) If no notice is given under paragraph (4) of this rule with respect to any such scheme, or such notice having been given, the scheme is approved by the General Synod, it shall come into operation on the day after the end of the group of sessions during which it was laid before, or approved by, the General Synod or on such later date as may be specified in the scheme.

REPRESENTATION OF CATHEDRAL CLERGY AND LAITY

22. (1) Any diocesan synod may provide by scheme for the representation on such deanery synod as may be determined by or under the scheme—

(*a*) of the dean or provost, the residentiary canons and other ministers of the cathedral church of the diocese, or any of them; and

(*b*) of lay persons who

(i) in a parish church cathedral are on the electoral roll prepared under rule 1 (1); or

> > (ii) in any other cathedral are declared by the dean to be habitual worshippers at the cathedral church of the diocese and whose names are not entered on the roll of any parish.

(2) Paragraph (2) of the last preceding rule shall apply to schemes made under this rule.

PROCEDURE

23. (1) The diocesan synod shall make rules for deanery synods which shall provide—

> (*a*) that the rural dean and a member of the house of laity elected by that house shall be joint chairmen of the deanery synod and that they shall agree between them who shall chair each meeting of the synod or particular items of business on the agenda of the synod;
> (*b*) that there shall be a secretary of the deanery synod;
> (*c*) that a specified minimum number of meetings shall be held by the deanery synod in each year;
> (*d*) that on such matters and in such circumstances as may be specified in the rules, voting shall be by houses, but that otherwise decisions shall be taken by a majority of the members of the synod present and voting;
> (*e*) that there shall be a standing committee of the synod with such membership and functions as the rules may provide;
> (*f*) that the synod shall prepare and circulate to all parochial church councils in the deanery a report of its proceedings;

and may provide for such other matters consistent with these rules as the diocesan synod think fit.

(2) Subject to any such rules, the deanery synod shall have power to determine its own procedure.

MEMBERSHIP OF DIOCESAN SYNODS

24. (1) A diocesan synod shall consist of a house of bishops, a house of clergy and a house of laity.

(1A) The members of the house of bishops shall consist of the bishop of the diocese, every suffragan bishop of the diocese and such other person or persons, being a person or persons in episcopal orders working in the diocese, as the bishop of the diocese, with the concurrence of the archbishop of the province, may nominate.

(1B) The bishop of the diocese shall be the president of the diocesan synod.

(2) The members of the house of clergy shall consist of—

(*a*) the following ex-officio members, that is to say—
  (i) any person or persons in episcopal orders nomi-nated by the bishop of the diocese, other than a suffragan bishop or a person nominated under para-graph (1A) of this rule;
  (ii) the dean or provost of the cathedral (including in appropriate dioceses, the Dean of Westminster, the Dean of Windsor and the Dean of Jersey and Guernsey);
  (iii) the archdeacons;
  (iv) the proctors elected from the diocese or from any university in the diocese (the University of London being treated for this purpose as being wholly in the diocese of London) to the Lower House of the Convocation of the Province, excluding the registrar of the diocese (if so elected);
  (v) any other member of that House, being the person chosen by and from among the clerical members of religious communities in the Province, who resides in the diocese;

(vi) the chancellor of the diocese (if in Holy Orders); and

(vii) the chairman of the diocesan board of finance (if in Holy Orders);

(*b*) members elected by the houses of clergy of the deanery synods in the diocese in accordance with the next following rules; and

(*c*) not more than five members (being clerks in Holy Orders) co-opted by the house of clergy of the diocesan synod.

(3) The members of the house of laity shall consist of—

(*a*) the following ex-officio members, that is to say—
   (i) the chancellor of the diocese (if not in Holy Orders);
   (ii) the chairman of the diocesan board of finance (if not in Holy Orders);
   (iii) the members elected from the diocese to the House of Laity of the General Synod, excluding the registrar of the diocese (if so elected);
   (iv) any other member of that House, being an ex-officio or co-opted member of the House of Laity of the General Synod or a person chosen by and from among the lay members of religious communities in the Province, who resides in the diocese;

(*b*) members elected by the houses of laity of the deanery synods in the diocese in accordance with the next following rules; and

(*c*) not more than five members co-opted by the house of laity of the diocesan synod, who shall be actual communicant members of the Church of England of eighteen years or upwards.

(4) The bishop of the diocese may nominate ten additional members of the diocesan synod, who may be of the clergy or the laity and shall be members of the appropriate house. Except in regard to their appointment the nominated members shall have the same rights and be subject to the same rules as elected members. Where necessary the bishop's council and standing committee shall designate the deanery synod of which the

nominated member shall be a member and, where a nominated lay person is on more than one electoral roll, he shall choose the parochial church council of which he is to be a member.

(5) No person, other than the chancellor of a diocese, shall be entitled to be a member of more than one diocesan synod at the same time.

ELECTIONS OF MEMBERS OF DIOCESAN SYNODS BY DEANERY SYNODS

25. (1) The elections of members of the diocesan synods by the houses of clergy and laity of the deanery synods in the diocese shall take place every three years, and the members so elected shall hold office for a term of three years beginning with the 1st August next following their election.

(2) Any clerk in Holy Orders who is a member of the deanery synod or is working or residing in the deanery shall be qualified to be so elected by the house of clergy of a deanery synod, and the electors shall be the members of that house other than the co-opted members:
Provided that no clerk shall stand for election by more than one deanery synod.

(3) Subject to the provisions of rule 1 (3), any lay person who is an actual communicant member of the Church of England of eighteen years or upwards and whose name is entered on the roll of any parish in the deanery or who is a lay person declared by the dean to be an habitual worshipper at the cathedral church of the diocese and to be associated with the deanery, shall be qualified to be so elected by the house of laity of a deanery synod, and the electors shall be the members of that house other than the co-opted members.

(4) The diocesan synod shall, not later than the 31st December in the year preceding any such election, determine the numbers of members to be so elected by the houses of the several deanery synods in the diocese, and the numbers shall—

(*a*) in the case of elections by the houses of clergy, be related to the numbers of members of those houses in the respective deanery synods;

(*b*) in the case of elections by the houses of laity, be related to the total numbers of names on the rolls of the parishes in the respective deaneries as certified under rule 4:

Provided that at least two members shall be elected by each house of every deanery synod.

(5) For the purpose of such determination by the diocesan synod, the secretary of every deanery synod shall, not later than the 1st July in the year preceding any such election, certify the number of members of the house of clergy of the synod to the secretary of the diocesan synod.

(6) The diocesan synod shall so exercise their powers under this rule as to secure that the number of members of the synod is not less than 150 and not more than 270 and that the numbers of the two houses are approximately equal.

For the avoidance of doubt it is hereby declared that the number 270 specified in this paragraph includes the maximum number of members who may be co-opted by each house or nominated by the bishop.

(7) Not later than the 31st December in each year preceding any such elections, the secretary of the diocesan synod shall certify to the secretary of every deanery synod the numbers determined under this rule for that deanery synod.

26. (1) Elections of members of the diocesan synod by the houses of the deanery synods shall be carried out in each diocese during such period between the 1st day of May and the 15th day of July (both inclusive) as shall be fixed by the bishop of the diocese and such period and dates fixed shall be communicated to the secretaries of the deanery synods.

(2) The presiding officers for the deaneries in each diocese shall be appointed by the bishop, and the expenses of elections shall be paid out of diocesan funds.

(3) Every candidate must be nominated and seconded by a qualified elector. A notice in the form set out in section 5 of Appendix I indicating the number of seats to be filled and inviting nominations shall be despatched to every elector by the presiding officer not earlier than 1st May in each election year. Nominations in the form set out in section 6 of Appendix I shall be sent to the presiding officer in writing within such period not being less than 14 days as he shall specify and be accompanied by a statement signed by the candidate of his willingness to serve.

(4) If more candidates are nominated than there are seats to be filled the names of the candidates nominated shall be circulated on a voting paper in the form set out in either section 7 or in section 8 of Appendix I to every qualified elector. The diocesan synod shall, not later than the 31st December in each year preceding any such election as is referred to in rule 25, make a determination as to which form of voting paper is to be used by the deaneries in that election, and that determination shall apply to any election to fill a casual vacancy which occurs during the next ensuing three years.

(5) The voting paper marked and, on the reverse thereof, signed by the elector and with his full name written shall be returnable to the presiding officer within such period not being less than fourteen days as he shall specify. No vote shall be counted if given on a voting paper not in accordance with this paragraph.

(6) Where voting papers in the form set out in section 7 of Appendix I have been used and owing to an equality of votes an election is not decided, the decision between the persons for whom the equal number of votes have been cast shall be taken by lot by the presiding officer.

(7) Where voting papers in the form set out in section 8 of Appendix I are used, the election shall be conducted under rules, with the necessary modifications, made by the General Synod under rule 33 (4) and for the time being in force.

(8) A return of the result of the election shall be sent by the presiding officer to the secretary of the diocesan synod and a statement of the result shall be sent by the presiding officer to every candidate not later than the 1st August in each election year.

VARIATION OF MEMBERSHIP OF DIOCESAN SYNODS BY SCHEME

27. (1) If it appears to the diocesan synod that the preceding rules in this Part relating to the membership of diocesan synods ought to be varied to meet the special circumstances of the diocese and to secure better representation of clergy or laity or both on the diocesan synod, they may make a scheme for such variation, and if the scheme comes into operation in accordance with the provisions hereinafter applied, the said rules shall have effect subject to the scheme.

Paragraphs (2) to (5) of rule 21 shall apply to schemes under this rule as it applies to schemes under that rule.

PROCEDURE OF DIOCESAN SYNODS

28. (1) The diocesan synod shall make standing orders which shall provide—

(*a*) that the bishop need not be chairman of its meetings if and to the extent that standing orders otherwise provide;

(*b*) that there shall be a secretary of the diocesan synod;

(*c*) that a specified minimum number of meetings being in the case of a diocese in which area synods have been constituted in accordance with section 17 of the Dioceses Measure 1978, not less than one, and in the case of any other diocese not less than two shall be held in each year;

(*d*) that a meeting of the diocesan synod shall be held if not less than a specified number of members of the synod so request;

(*e*) that subject to the three next following sub-paragraphs, nothing shall be deemed to have the assent of the diocesan synod unless the three houses which constitute the synod have assented thereto, but that if in the case of a particular question (except a matter referred to the diocesan synod by the General Synod under the provisions of Article 8 of the Constitution) the diocesan bishop (if present) so directs, that question shall be deemed to have the assent of the house of bishops only if the majority of the members of that house who assent thereto includes the diocesan bishop;

(*f*) that questions relating only to the conduct of business shall be decided by the votes of all the members of the diocesan synod present and voting;

(*g*) that every other question shall be decided by the votes of all the members of the diocesan synod present and voting, the assent of the three houses being presumed, unless the diocesan bishop (if present) requires or any ten members require that a separate vote of each house be taken;

(*h*) that if the votes of the houses of clergy and laity are in favour of any matter referred to the diocesan synod by the General Synod under the provisions of Article 8 of Schedule 2 of this Measure, that matter shall be deemed to have been approved for the purposes of the said Article;

(*i*) that where there is an equal division of votes in the house of bishops, the diocesan bishop shall have a second or casting vote;

(*j*) that the diocesan bishop shall have a right to require that his opinion on any question shall be recorded in the minutes;

(*k*) that there shall be a bishop's council and standing committee of the diocesan synod with such membership as may be provided by standing orders and with the functions exercisable by it under section 4 (4) of the Measure and such other functions as may be provided by the standing orders or by these rules or by any Measure or Canon;

and may contain such further provisions consistent with these rules as the diocesan synod shall consider appropriate.

(2) No person shall be entitled to serve as a member of more than one bishop's council and standing committee at the same time.

(3) The registrar of the diocese shall be the registrar of the diocesan synod, and may appoint a deputy.

PART V HOUSE OF LAITY OF GENERAL SYNOD

MEMBERSHIP OF HOUSE OF LAITY

29. (1) The House of Laity of the General Synod shall consist of—

(*a*) the members elected by the diocesan electors of each diocese as hereinafter provided;

(*b*) three members, two from the Province of Canterbury and one from the Province of York, chosen by the lay members of religious communities from among their number in such manner as may be provided by a resolution of the General Synod;

(*c*) such ex-officio and co-opted members as are hereinafter provided.

(1A) For the purposes of this Part of these rules the diocese in Europe shall be deemed to be a diocese in the province of Canterbury.

(2) For the purposes of this Part of these rules, the diocesan electors of a diocese other than the diocese in Europe shall be the members of the houses of laity of all the deanery synods in the diocese other than the co-opted members.

(3) The diocesan electors of the diocese in Europe shall be such number of persons elected by the annual meetings of the chaplaincies in the said diocese as may be determined by the bishop's council and standing committee of the said diocese, and any lay person who is:

(*a*) an actual communicant member of the Church of England or of a Church in communion with the Church;

(*b*) of eighteen years or upwards; and

(*c*) a person whose name is entered on the electoral roll of such a chaplaincy;

shall be qualified for election as a diocesan elector by the annual meeting of that chaplaincy.

Number of Elected Members

30. (1) the total number of members directly elected and specially elected from the dioceses in the Province shall not exceed 170 for Canterbury and 80 for York and no diocese shall have fewer than three directly elected members (except the diocese in Europe which shall elect two members, and the diocese of Sodor and Man which shall elect one member). Ex-officio and co-opted members (as defined in rule 35) shall be additional to the said total number.

In this rule the term 'specially elected' means the representatives of the religious communities referred to in rule 29 (1) hereof and the representatives of the Channel Islands elected in accordance with the provisions of the Channel Islands (Representation) Measure 1931 and such persons shall be included in the said total number.

(1A) The total number of members to be elected by the diocesan electors of all the dioceses shall be fixed by resolution of the General Synod not later than the last day of November in the fourth year after the last preceding election of the House of Laity (but subject as hereinafter provided), and the resolution shall apportion the number so fixed to the Provinces of Canterbury and York in a proportion of 68 to 32 or as nearly as possible thereto and shall divide the number among the dioceses so that the number of members to be elected by the several dioceses are as nearly as possible proportionate to the total number of names certified for them under the following paragraph.

(2) The secretary of each diocesan synod shall, not later than the 1st August in the fourth year after the last preceding election of the House of Laity, certify to the secretary of the General

Synod the total number of names on the rolls of the parishes of the diocese.

(3) The number of members of the House of Laity to be elected by each diocese, when fixed by the General Synod as aforesaid, shall forthwith be certified to the secretaries of the diocesan synods.

(4) If the General Synod is at any time dissolved before the fourth year after the last preceding election of the House of Laity or before the fixing of numbers under this rule by the General Synod during that year, the General Synod or the Presidents thereof may give directions with respect to the fixing and certifying of the numbers of members to be elected to the House of Laity by each diocese, and the directions may provide that the numbers so fixed and certified on the last previous occasion shall be deemed to have been fixed and certified for the purpose of the election following the dissolution, and the directions may, if the dissolution is known to be impending, be given before it occurs.

Qualifications of Elected Members

31. (1) Subject to the provisions of rule 1 (3) and of paragraphs (1A) and (1B) of this rule, a lay person shall be qualified for election for any diocese by the diocesan electors of the diocese if—

(*a*) he is an actual communicant member of the Church of England;
(*b*) he is of eighteen years of age on the date of the dissolution of the General Synod;
(*c*) his name is at 6.00 a.m. on the date of dissolution of the General Synod entered on the roll of any parish in the diocese or who at any time within the period of two months beginning one month immediately before that date is declared by the dean of the cathedral church to be an habitual worshipper at that cathedral church.

(1A) Subject to the provisions of rule 1 (3) and of paragraph

(1B) of this rule, any lay person who is an actual communicant member of the Church of England or of a Church in communion with that Church and of eighteen years or upwards whose name is entered on the electoral roll of any chaplaincy in the diocese of Europe shall be qualified for election by the diocesan electors of that diocese.

(1B) A person shall be disqualified from being nominated for election as a member of the General Synod if he holds any paid office or employment appointment to which is or may be made or confirmed by the General Synod, the Convocations, the Central Board of Finance, the Church Commissioners for England (except that such disqualification shall not apply to any Commissioner so appointed in receipt of a salary or other emoluments), the Church of England Pensions Board or the Corporation of the Church House.

(2) Where a diocese is divided into two or more areas in accordance with rule 32 (2), any person who under this rule is qualified for election for the diocese shall be qualified for election for any such area whether or not the parish on whose roll his name is entered, or the cathedral church at which he is an habitual worshipper, is situated in that area, but no person shall be nominated for more than one such area at the same time.

Electoral Areas

32. (1) Subject to any division of a diocese under this rule every diocese shall be an electoral area for the purposes of elections to the House of Laity.

(2) So far as is consistent with any rule made under the Standing Orders of the General Synod under paragraph (4) of the next following rule and subject to paragraph (3) of this rule, a diocesan synod may, for the purposes of any election, divide a diocese into two or more areas, and apportion the number of members of the House of Laity to be elected for the diocese among such areas, and the election shall be conducted in each area as if such area were a separate diocese. Where a diocese

is so divided, a diocesan elector who is a representative of the laity shall vote in the area to which the body by which he was elected belongs, and a diocesan elector who is not a representative of the laity shall vote in such area as the diocesan synod may decide. Any such division shall remain in force until it is revoked by the diocesan synod.

(3) If a diocesan synod decide to divide the diocese into two or more areas in pursuance of this rule the division shall be made in such manner that the number of members to be elected in any such area will be not less than three.

Conduct of Elections

33. (1) Subject to any directions by the General Synod or the Presidents thereof, elections to the House of Laity shall be carried out during the three months immediately following any dissolution of the General Synod and shall be so carried out in each diocese during such period within the said three months as shall be fixed by the archbishops of Canterbury and York.

(2) The presiding officer in each diocese or each area of a diocese shall be the registrar of the diocese or a person appointed by him with the approval of the registrar of the province, except that, if the said registrar is a candidate in the election, the presiding officer shall be a person appointed by the registrar of the province. The expenses of the elections shall be paid out of diocesan funds.

(3) Every candidate must be nominated and seconded by diocesan electors qualified to vote in the area in which the candidate is seeking to be elected. All nominations shall be in writing, shall include the year of the candidate's birth and shall be sent to the presiding officer of the area, together with evidence of the candidate's consent to serve, within such period, being a period of not less than twenty-eight days ending on a date specified by the presiding officer, as that officer may specify. If any of the candidates so request the presiding officer shall despatch to every elector election addresses from those can-

didates, sufficient copies of the addresses to be provided by the candidates at their own expense and to be delivered to the presiding officer by such date as he shall determine being not less than seven days after the close of nominations. The presiding officer shall be under no obligation to despatch to electors election addresses received after the due date.

(4) If more candidates are nominated for any area than there are seats to be filled, the election shall be conducted by voting papers by the method of the single transferable vote under rules to be made from time to time as provided by the Standing Orders of the General Synod. Every voting paper, which shall include the year of birth of each candidate, shall be marked and signed on the reverse thereof by the elector and shall be returnable to the presiding officer within such period, being a period of not less than twenty-one days after the date on which the voting paper is issued, as that officer may specify.

(5) A candidate or a person nominated by him has the right to be present at, but shall take no part in, the counting of the votes, and the presiding officer of the area shall give notice to each candidate of the time and place at which the votes are to be counted.

(6) A full statement of the result of each election shall be furnished to every candidate within the area, and published in such manner as the bishop may approve.

(7) The presiding officer in each area shall ensure that the valid voting papers received by him for the purposes of any election to the House of Laity are preserved for a period of not less than two years beginning with the date of the election.

Duties and Payment of Presiding Officers

33A. (1) Rules defining the duties to be undertaken by the presiding officers in connection with elections to the House of Laity shall be prepared by the provincial registrars acting jointly, but no such rules shall have effect unless approved by the Standing Committee of the General Synod.

(2) A presiding officer shall be entitled to such fees for the performance by him of the duties aforesaid as may be specified in any order for the time being in force made under section 1 of the Ecclesiastical Fees Measure 1962; and where with the prior agreement in writing of the bishop's council and standing committee the presiding officer or any other person performs any other duties in connection with elections to the House of Laity he shall be entitled to such fees as may be specified in the agreement.

Term of Office of Elected and Representative Members

34. The term of office of elected members of the House of Laity and of members chosen by the lay members of religious communities shall be for the lifetime of the General Synod for which they are elected or chosen, but without prejudice to their acting under Article 3 (4) of the Constitution during the period of the dissolution of the General Synod or as ex-officio members of other bodies constituted under these rules during that period.

EX-OFFICIO AND CO-OPTED MEMBERS OF THE HOUSE OF LAITY

35. (1) The following persons, if they are not in Holy Orders, shall be ex-officio members of the House of Laity—

(*a*) the Dean of the Arches and Auditor;
(*b*) the Vicar-General of the Province of Canterbury;
(*c*) the Vicar-General of the Province of York;
(*d*) the three Church Estates Commissioners;
(*e*) the Chairman of the Central Board of Finance.

(2) The House of Laity shall have power to co-opt persons who are actual lay communicant members of the Church of England of eighteen years or upwards to be members of the House of Laity:
Provided that—

(*a*) the co-opted members shall not at any time exceed five in number; and (*b*) no person shall be qualified to become a co-opted member unless not less than two-thirds of the members of the Standing Committee of the House of Laity shall have first consented to his being co-opted, either at a meeting of the Standing Committee or in writing.

(3) Except in regard to their appointment, the ex-officio and co-opted members shall have the same rights and be subject to the same rules and regulations as elected members. Where such members are on more than one electoral roll, they shall choose the parochial church council of which they are to be a member.

(4) Co-opted members shall continue to be members of the House of Laity until the next dissolution of the General Synod, but without prejudice to their acting under Article 3 (4) of the Constitution during the period of the dissolution:
Provided that the House of Laity may, in the case of any co-opted member, fix a shorter period of membership.

(5) The House of Laity may make standing orders for regulating the procedure of and incidental to the appointment of co-opted members and otherwise for carrying this rule into effect.

PART VI APPEALS AND DISQUALIFICATIONS

APPEALS

36. (1) There shall be a right of appeal by any person aggrieved against—

(*a*) any enrolment, or refusal of enrolment, on the roll of a parish;
(*b*) the removal of any name, or the refusal to remove any name, from the roll of a parish;
(*c*) the allowance or disallowance of any vote given or tendered in an election of a churchwarden or in an election under these rules or to a body constituted under or in accordance with these rules;
(*d*) the result of any election of a churchwarden or of any

election or choice held or made or purporting to be held or made under these rules, or any election or choice of members of a body constituted under or in accordance with these rules.

(1A) The provisions of this rule (except paragraph (3)), insofar as they confer a right of appeal by any person aggrieved against the result of an election and provide for notice of an appeal and the determination thereof, shall apply in relation to an election to the House of Laity of the General Synod by the diocesan electors of the diocese in Europe.

(2) In the case of an appeal arising out of an election to the House of Laity of the General Synod or the diocesan synod or the choosing of a retired clerk in Holy Orders in accordance with rule 19 (2) (*e*), notice of the appeal shall be given in writing to the bishop. In any other case, notice of the appeal shall be given in writing to the lay chairman of the deanery synod. Notices under this paragraph shall be given:

(*a*) in the case of an appeal against an enrolment or a refusal of enrolment, or in the case of an appeal against the removal of any name or the refusal to remove any name from the roll, not later than fourteen days after the date of the enrolment, removal or refusal or if the appeal arises on the revision of the roll or the preparation of a new roll, not later than fourteen days after the first publication of the revised or new roll under rule 2 (3) or (7);

(*b*) in the case of an appeal against the allowance or disallowance of a vote, not later than fourteen days after such allowance or disallowance;

(*c*) in the case of an appeal against the result of an election, not later than fourteen days after the result thereof has been announced by the presiding officer.

(3) An error in the electoral roll shall not be a ground of appeal against the result of any election unless—

(*a*) either it has been determined under this rule that there has been such an error or the question is awaiting determination under this rule; and (*b*) the error would or might be material to the result of the election;

and the allowance or disallowance of a vote shall not be a ground of appeal against the result of an election unless the allowance or disallowance would or might be material to the result of the election.

(3A) An error in the electoral roll of a chaplaincy in the diocese in Europe shall not be a ground of appeal against the result of an election to the House of Laity of the General Synod by the diocesan electors of that diocese unless—

(*a*) either it has been determined under the rule which applies in that diocese and corresponds with this rule that there has been such an error or the question is awaiting determination under that rule; and
(*b*) the error would or might be material to the result of that election;

and the allowance or disallowance of a vote shall not be a ground of appeal against the result of such an election unless the allowance or disallowance would or might be material to the result of the election.

(4) An appeal arising out of an election or choice of members of the House of Laity of the General Synod shall, unless the parties agree to a settlement of their dispute, be referred by the bishop to the Standing Committee of the Synod who shall appoint three or a greater number, being an odd numer, of their lay members to consider and decide the appeal. The decision of such members shall be final.

(5) In an appeal arising under this rule except an appeal arising out of an election to the House of Laity of the General Synod, the bishop or the lay chairman of the deanery synod, as the case may be, shall, unless the parties agree to a settlement of their dispute, refer any appeal to the bishop's council and standing committee of the diocese who, in an appeal concerning an election of the House of Clergy of the diocesan synod, shall

appoint three or a greater number being an odd number of their clerical members to consider and decide the appeal and, in an appeal concerning lay persons, the bishop's council and standing committee shall appoint three or a greater number being an odd number of their lay members to consider and decide the appeal. Their decision shall be final.

(6) For the purpose of the consideration and decision of any appeal under this rule, the members of the Standing Committee or the bishop's council, as the case may be, shall consider all the relevant circumstances, and shall be entitled to inspect all documents and papers relating to the subject matter of the appeal, and be furnished with all information respecting the same which they may require. They shall give to the parties to the appeal an opportunity of appearing before them in person or through a legal or other representative.

(7) The members of the Standing Committee or the bishop's council, as the case may be, shall have power at any time to extend the time within which a notice of appeal is given.

VACATION OF SEAT BY MEMBER CEASING TO BE QUALIFIED FOR ELECTION

37. (1) Where—

(*a*) any lay member of a deanery synod, being a parochial representative or a representative under rule 22, ceases to be entered on the roll of the parish by which he was elected or, as the case may be, to be declared under the said rule to be an habitual worshipper at the cathedral church;

(*b*) any member of a diocesan synod elected by the house of clergy of a deanery synod ceases to be qualified for election by that house;

(*c*) any lay member of a diocesan synod elected by the house of laity of a deanery synod ceases to have the qualification of entry on the roll of any parish in that deanery or (in appropriate cases) of being declared an habitual worshipper at the cathedral church of the diocese under rule 22;

(*d*) any elected member of the House of Laity of the General Synod ceases to have the qualification of entry on the roll of any parish in the diocese for which he was elected or of being declared an habitual worshipper as aforesaid;

(*e*) any elected member of the House of Laity of the General Synod takes any paid office or employment as provided by rule 31 (1B);

his seat shall, subject to the following provisions of this rule, forthwith be vacated.

(2) If the name of a person to whom paragraph 1 (*a*) of the rule applies is entered on the roll of any parish in the diocese other than that of the parish mentioned in (1) (*a*) above or if he is declared under rule 22 to be an habitual worshipper at the cathedral church of the diocese, his seat shall not be vacated under this rule if, before the vacancy occurs, the parochial church council so resolve.

(3) If a person to whom paragraph (1) (*b*) of this rule applies continues to work or reside in the diocese, his seat shall not be vacated under this rule if, before the vacancy occurs, the clerical members of the standing committee of the deanery synod so resolve.

(4) If the name of a person to whom paragraph (1) (*c*) of this rule applies is entered on the roll of any parish in the diocese other than that of the parish mentioned in (1) (*c*) above or if he is declared under rule 22 to be an habitual worshipper at the cathedral church of the diocese, his seat shall not be vacated under this rule if, before the vacancy occurs, the lay members of the standing committee of the deanery synod so resolve.

(5) If the lay members of the bishop's council and standing committee have determined before the vacancy occurs that a person to whom paragraph (1) (*d*) of this rule applies should remain a member of the House of Laity, neither his seat as a member of that House nor his seat as a lay member of the diocesan synod shall be vacated under this rule.

(6) This rule shall apply in relation to a member of the House of Laity of the General Synod elected for the diocese in Europe with the substitution for the words in paragraph (1) (*d*) from 'roll' to 'aforesaid' of the words 'electoral roll of any chaplaincy in that diocese'.

Ex-Officio Membership not to Disqualify for Election

38.   No person shall be disqualified from being elected or chosen a member of any body under these rules by the fact that he is also a member ex-officio of that body; and no person shall be deemed to vacate his seat as such an elected or chosen member of any body by reason only of the fact that subsequently to his election or choice he has become a member of that body ex-officio.

PART VII SUPPLEMENTARY AND INTERPRETATION

CASUAL VACANCIES

39.   (1) Where a casual vacancy among the parochial representatives elected to the parochial church council or deanery synod occurs the vacancy may be filled by the election by the parochial church council of a person qualified to be so elected.

(2) Where a casual vacancy among the members of a diocesan synod elected by either house of a deanery synod occurs, the vacancy may be filled by the election by that house of a person qualified to be so elected, and a meeting of the members of that house who are electors may be held for that purpose.

(3) Subject to paragraphs (1), (2) and (6) of this rule, casual vacancies among persons elected under these rules shall be filled by elections conducted in the same manner as ordinary elections.

(4) Elections to fill casual vacancies shall, where possible, be held at such times as will enable all casual vacancies among representatives of the laity who are electors to be filled at the time of every election to the House of Laity of the General

Synod, but no such election shall be invalid by reason of any casual vacancies not having been so filled.

(5) Elections to fill casual vacancies shall be held as soon as reasonably practicable after the vacancy has occurred, and elections to fill a casual vacancy in the House of Laity of the General Synod or either house of the diocesan synod shall be completed within six months from the occurrence of the vacancy. In the event of a casual vacancy in the House of Laity of the General Synod not being filled within six months of the occurrence of the vacancy, the vacancy shall remain unfilled until the next general election of the House of Laity:

Provided that where a casual vacancy occurs in any of these three houses and the period for holding a general election to that house is due to begin, in the case of a general election to the House of Laity, within twelve months of the vacancy, and, in the case of a general election to either house of the diocesan synod, within nine months of the vacancy, the vacancy shall not be filled unless, in the first-mentioned case, the bishop's council and standing committee, acting in accordance with any directions of the diocesan synod, otherwise direct or, in the last-mentioned case, the bishop otherwise directs.

(6) If a casual vacancy in the House of Laity of the General Synod occurs within the period of two years beginning with 1st August in the year of the last general election to that House or the date of any subsequent declaration of the result of an election to fill a casual vacancy and that election was conducted by voting papers by the method of the single transferable vote in the same manner as a general election, then, provided that within three months of the occurrence of the vacancy the bishop's council and standing committee, acting in accordance with any directions of the diocesan synod, so decide, the election to fill the casual vacancy shall be conducted by those papers in accordance with paragraph (7) of this rule.

(7) The presiding officer for the area in question shall ask every candidate not elected in the preceding election who is still qualified for election for the diocese in question if he

consents to serve. If there is only one such candidate and he so consents or only one of those candidates so consents he shall be elected to fill the casual vacancy. If two or more of those candidates so consent the votes validly cast in the preceding election shall be recounted from the beginning in accordance with the rules mentioned in rule 33 (4):

Provided that no continuing candidate elected during the original count shall be excluded.

(8) The preceding provisions of this rule shall apply, so far as applicable and with the necessary modifications, to the choosing of persons under these rules as it applies to the election of persons thereunder, and shall also apply to the election or choosing of members of any body constituted under or in accordance with these rules.

(9) Any person elected or chosen to fill a casual vacancy shall hold office only for the unexpired portion of the term of office of the person in whose place he is elected or chosen.

(10) This rule shall apply in relation to the filling of a casual vacancy among the members of the House of Laity of the General Synod elected for the diocese in Europe with the omission of the words in paragraph (5) and (6) 'acting in accordance with any directions of the diocesan synod'.

RESIGNATIONS

40. Any person holding any office under these rules or being a member of any body constituted by or under these rules may resign his office or membership by notice in writing signed by him and sent or given to the secretary of the body of which he is an officer or member, as the case may be; and his resignation shall take effect on the date specified in the notice or, if no date is so specified, on the receipt of the notice by the secretary of that body.

NOTICES

41. Any notice or other document required or authorised to be sent or given under these rules shall be deemed to have been duly sent or given if sent through the post addressed to the person to whom it is required or authorised to be sent or given at that person's last known address.

REVOCATION AND VARIATION OF RULES, ETC.

42. Subject to the provisions of these rules any power conferred by these rules to make, approve, frame, pass or adopt any rule, resolution, determination, decision, appointment or scheme, or to give any consent or settle any constitution, or to prescribe the manner of doing anything, shall be construed as including a power, exercisable in a like manner and subject to the like conditions, to revoke or vary any such rule, order, resolution, determination, decision, appointment, scheme, consent or constitution, or anything so prescribed.

SPECIAL PROVISIONS

43. (1) In the carrying out of these rules in any diocese the bishop of such diocese shall have power—

(*a*) to make provision for any matter not herein provided for;
(*b*) to appoint a person to do any act in respect of which there has been any neglect or default on the part of any person or body charged with any duty under these rules;
(*c*) so far as may be necessary for the purpose of giving effect to the intention of these rules, to extend or alter the time for holding any meeting or election or to modify the procedure laid down by these rules in connection therewith, provided that such power shall not be exercised in relation to the conduct of the elections referred to in rules 33 and 39 of these rules;
(*d*) in any case in which there has been no valid election, to direct a fresh election to be held and to give such directions in connection therewith as he may think necessary; and

(*e*) in any case in which any difficulties arise, to give any directions which he may consider expedient for the purpose of removing the difficulties.

(2) The powers of the bishop under this rule shall not enable him—

(*a*) to validate anything that was invalid at the time when it was done;
(*b*) to give any direction that is contrary to any resolution of the General Synod.

(3) No proceedings of any body constituted under these rules shall be invalidated by any vacancy in the membership of that body or by any defect in the qualification, election or appointment of any members thereof.

(4) No proceedings shall be invalidated by the use of a form which differs from that prescribed by these rules if the form which has in fact been used is to a substantially similar effect. Any question as to whether the form which has been used is to a substantially similar effect shall be determined by the bishop.

(5) In the case of an omission in any parish to prepare or maintain a roll or form or maintain a council or to hold the annual meeting, the rural dean, upon such omission being brought to his notice, shall ascertain and report to the bishop the cause thereof.

(6) During a vacancy in an archbishopric or where by reason of illness an archbishop is unable to exercise his functions under these rules or to appoint a commissary under paragraph (10) of this rule the functions of an archbishop under these rules shall be exercisable by the other archbishop.

(7) During a vacancy in a diocesan bishopric the functions of a diocesan bishop under these rules, including his functions as president of the diocesan synod, shall be exercisable by such person, being a person in episcopal orders, as the archbishop of the province may appoint.

(8) Where by reason of illness a diocesan bishop is unable to exercise his functions under these rules or to appoint a commissary under paragraph (10) of this rule, the archbishop of the province may, if he thinks it necessary or expedient to do so, appoint a person in episcopal orders to exercise the functions mentioned in paragraph (7) of this rule during the period of the bishop's illness.

(9) If a person appointed in pursuance of paragraph (7) or (8) of this rule becomes unable by reason of illness to act under the appointment, the archbishop may revoke the appointment and make a fresh one.

(10) An archbishop or diocesan bishop may appoint a commissary and delegate to him all or any of the functions of the archbishop or bishop under these rules, but if a bishop proposes to delegate to a commissary his functions as president of the diocesan synod he shall appoint a person in episcopal orders as commissary.

(11) If a person appointed in pursuance of paragraph (7) or (8) of this rule, or a person to whom the functions of a bishop as president of the diocesan synod are delegated under paragraph (10) thereof, is a member of the house of clergy of the diocesan synod, his membership of that house shall be suspended during the period for which the appointment or delegation has effect.

(12) The preceding provisions of this rule shall have effect in the diocese in Europe as if the references therein to these rules were references to such of these rules as apply in that diocese, and subject to paragraph (6) of this rule, the powers of an archbishop under this rule shall, as respects that diocese, be exercisable by the Archbishop of Canterbury.

MEANING OF MINISTER, PARISH AND OTHER WORDS AND PHRASES

44. (1) In these rules—

'actual communicant member of the Church of England' means

a member of the Church of England who is confirmed or ready and desirous of being confirmed and has received Communion according to the use of the Church of England or of a Church in communion with the Church of England at least three times during the twelve months preceding the date of his election or appointment;

'actual communicant member of a Church in communion with the Church of England' means a communicant member of a Church in communion with the Church of England who has received Communion according to the use of the Church of England or of a Church in communion with the Church of England at least three times during the twelve months preceding the date of his election or appointment;

'the Measure' means the Synodical Government Measure 1969;

'minister' means—

(*a*) the incumbent of a parish;

(*b*) a curate licensed to the charge of a parish or a minister acting as priest-in-charge of a parish in respect of which rights of presentation are suspended; and

(*c*) a vicar in a team ministry to the extent that the duties of a minister are assigned to him by a scheme under the Pastoral Measure 1968 or his licence from the bishop;

'parish' means—

(*a*) an ecclesiastical parish; and

(*b*) a district which is constituted a 'conventional district' for the cure of souls;

'public worship' means public worship according to the rites and ceremonies of the Church of England.

(2) Any reference in these rules to the laity shall be construed as a reference to persons other than clerks in Holy Orders, and the expression 'lay' in these rules shall be construed accordingly.

(3) Where a person has executed a deed of relinquishment under the Clerical Disabilities Act 1870 and the deed has been enrolled in the High Court and recorded in the registry of a

diocese under that Act then, unless and until the vacation of the enrolment of the deed is recorded in such a registry under the Clerical Disabilities Act 1870 (Amendment) Measure 1934, that person shall be deemed not to be a clerk in Holy Orders for the purpose of paragraph (2) above or of any other provision of these rules which refers to such a clerk.

(4) References in these rules to the cathedral church of the diocese shall include, in the case of the dioceses of London and Oxford, references to Westminster Abbey and St George's Chapel, Windsor, respectively.

(5) If any question arises whether a Church is a Church in communion with the Church of England, it shall be conclusively determined for the purposes of these rules by the Archbishops of Canterbury and York.

(6) In these rules words importing residence include residence of a regular nature but do not include residence of a casual nature.

(7) Any reference herein to 'these rules' shall be construed as including a reference to the Appendices hereto.

APPENDIX I

Section 1

Rule 1 (2)

APPLICATION FOR ENROLMENT ON CHURCH ELECTORAL ROLL

I ....
(Full Christian name and surname)

of ....
(Full postal address)

am baptised and am a member of the Church of England or of a Church in communion with it. I am sixteen years or over and am either resident in the parish or an habitual attender at public worship there for at least the past six months.

I apply for entry on the church electoral roll of the parish of
....

Signed ....

Date ....

NOTES

1. The only Churches at present in communion with the Church of England are other Anglican Churches and certain foreign Churches. Members of other Churches in England are usually admitted to communion as individuals, but their Churches are not yet in communion with the Church of England. Such persons would naturally take part in the government of their own Churches.

2. Every six years a new roll is prepared and those on the previous roll are informed so that they can re-apply. If you are not resident in the parish but were on the roll as an habitual

worshipper and have been prevented by sickness or absence or other essential reason from worshipping for the past six months, you may write 'would' before 'have habitually attended' in the form and add 'but was prevented from doing so because ...' and then state the reason.

3. If you have any problems over this form, please approach the clergy or lay people responsible for the parish, who will be pleased to help you.

4. In this form 'parish' means an ecclesiastical parish.

Section 2

Rule 2 (1)

FORM OF NOTICE OF REVISION OF CHURCH ELECTORAL ROLL

Diocese of ....

Parish of ....

Notice is hereby given that the Church Electoral Roll of the above parish will be revised by the Parochial Church Council,[1] beginning on .... the .... day of .... 19... and ending on .... the .... day of .... 19...

After such Revision, a copy of the roll will forthwith be exhibited on, or near to, the principal door of the Parish Church for inspection.

Under the Church Representation Rules any persons are entitled to have their names entered on the roll, if they—

(i) are baptised,

(ii) are members of the Church of England or of any Church in communion with the Church of England,

(iii) are sixteen or over,

(iv) are resident in the parish, or, not being resident in the parish, have habitually attended public worship in the parish during the six months before the date of application for enrolment, and

(v) have signed a form of application for enrolment.

Forms of application for enrolment can be obtained from the undersigned, and should be returned, if possible, in time for the Revision.

1 The Revision must be completed not less than 15 days or more than 28 days before the Annual Parochial Church Meeting.

Any error discovered in the roll should at once be reported to the undersigned.

Dated this[1] .... day of ....

19...

....
Church Electoral Roll Officer
Address ....

NOTE: In this notice 'parish' means an ecclesiastical parish.

1 Not less than 14 days notice must be given.

Section 3

Rule 2 (4)

FORM OF NOTICE OF PREPARATION OF NEW ROLL

Diocese of ....

Parish of ....

Notice is hereby given that under the Church Representation Rules a new Church Electoral Roll is being prepared.[1] All persons who wish to have their names entered on the new roll, whether their names are entered on the present roll or not, are requested to apply for enrolment if possible not later than

....

....

The new roll will come into operation on ....

....

Forms of application for enrolment can be obtained from the undersigned.

Under the Church Representation Rules any persons are entitled to have their names entered on the roll, if they—

(i) are baptised,

(ii) are members of the Church of England or of any Church in communion with the Church of England,

(iii) are sixteen or over,

(iv) are resident in the parish, or, not being resident in the parish, have habitually attended public worship in the parish during the six months before the date of application for enrolment, and

(v) have signed a form of application for enrolment.

Any error discovered in the roll should at once be reported to the undersigned.

1 The new roll must be completed not less than 15 days or more than 28 days before the Annual Parochial Church Meeting.

Dated this .... day of ....
19...

....
                    Church Electoral Roll Officer
                    Address ....

NOTE: In this notice 'parish' means an ecclesiastical parish.

Section 4

Rule 6 (1)

NOTICE OF ANNUAL PAROCHIAL CHURCH MEETING

Parish of ....

The Annual Parochial Church Meeting will be held in........

. . . .

on .... day of .... at ....

For the election of Parochial representatives of the laity as follows—

  To the Deanery Synod .... representatives.[1]
  To the Parochial Church Council .... representatives.

For the election of Sidesmen.
For the consideration of:

  (*a*) A copy or copies of the Roll;
  (*b*) An Annual Report of the proceedings of the Council;
  (*c*) An Annual Report on the financial affairs of the parish;
  (*d*) The audited Accounts of the Council for the year ending on the 31st December immediately preceding the meeting;
  (*e*) An audited Statement of the funds and property of the Council;
  (*f*) A Report upon the fabric, goods and ornaments of the church or churches of the parish;
  (*g*) A Report on the proceedings of the Deanery Synod;

and other matters of parochial or general Church interest.

All persons whose names are entered upon the Church Electoral Roll of the parish (and such persons only) are entitled to vote at the election of parochial representatives of the laity.

A person is qualified to be elected a parochial representative of the laity to the deanery synod if—

1 Include where applicable.

(*a*) his name is entered on the church electoral roll of the parish;

(*b*) he is a member of the Church of England who is confirmed or ready and desirous of being confirmed and has received Communion according to the use of the Church of England or a Church in communion with the Church of England at least three times during the twelve months preceding the date of the election; and

(*c*) he is of eighteen years or upwards.

A person is qualified to be elected a parochial representative of the laity to the parochial church council if—

(*a*) his name is entered on the church electoral roll of the parish;

(*b*) he is a member of the Church of England who is confirmed or ready and desirous of being confirmed or a communicant member of a Church in communion with the Church of England and has received Communion according to the use of the Church of England or a Church in communion with the Church of England at least three times during the twelve months preceding the date of the election; and

(*c*) he is of seventeen years or upwards.

Any person whose name is on the roll may be a sidesman.

Signed ....
Minister of the parish.[1]

NOTE: In this notice 'parish' means an ecclesiastical parish.

1 Or 'Vice-Chairman of the Parochical Church Council' as the case may be (see rule 6(3) of the Church Representation Rules).

Section 5

Rule 26 (3)

NOTICE OF ELECTION TO HOUSE OF CLERGY OR HOUSE OF LAITY
OF DIOCESAN SYNOD

Diocese of ....
Deanery of ....

1. An election of ... members of the House of Clergy/Laity
of the Diocesan Synod will be held in the above Deanery on
....

2. Candidates must be nominated and seconded by qualified
electors on forms to be obtained from ....

All members, other than co-opted members, of the House of
Clergy/Laity of the Deanery Synod are qualified electors.

3. The election will be decided by simple majority/the single
transferable vote.

4. Nominations must be received by no later than 12 o'clock
(noon) on ....

Date ....

Presiding Officer.

Section 6

Rule 26 (3)

FORM OF NOMINATION TO THE HOUSE OF CLERGY OR HOUSE OF
LAITY OF DIOCESAN SYNOD

Diocese of ....
Deanery of ....
Election of members of the House of Clergy/Laity of
the Diocesan Synod

We the undersigned, being qualified electors, hereby nominate the following person as a candidate at the election in the
above Deanery.

Surname	Christian Names	Address and Profession or Occupation

Proposer's signature ....
Proposer's full name ....
Address ....
Seconder's signature ....
Seconder's full name ....
Address ....

I, the above named .... hereby
signify my willingness to serve as a member of the House of
Clergy/Laity of the Diocesan Synod if elected.

Candidate's signature......................

Note: This nomination must be sent to..........................
so as to be received no later than 12 noon on ....

All members, other than co-opted members, of the House of Clergy/Laity of the Deanery Synod are qualified electors.

Section 7

Rule 26 (4)

FORM OF VOTING PAPER FOR ELECTIONS TO THE HOUSE OF CLERGY
OR THE HOUSE OF LAITY OF THE DIOCESAN SYNOD

...............................Diocesan Synod

Election of   members of the House of Clergy/Laity
Deanery of ....
...............................members to be elected.

Voting paper

Candidates' names, addresses and descriptions	Mark your vote in this column

Guidance to Voters

1. This voting paper must be signed, and the full name written on the reverse.

2. You have as many votes as there are members to be elected.

3. You may not give more than one vote to any one candidate.

4. You vote by placing an 'X' opposite the name(s) of the candidate(s) of your choice.

5. If you inadvertently spoil your voting paper you may return it to the Presiding Officer who will give you another paper.

6. This voting paper duly completed on the reverse thereof must be delivered (by post or otherwise) to.....................
so as to arrive by no later than ....

(to be printed on back of form)	Signature of Voter ....
	Full name....................................
	Address ....
	....

Section 8

Rule 26 (4)

FORM OF VOTING PAPER FOR ELECTIONS TO THE HOUSE OF CLERGY
OR THE HOUSE OF LAITY OF THE DIOCESAN SYNOD

................................Diocesan Synod

Election of   members of the House of Clergy/Laity
Deanery of ....
................................members to be elected.

Voting paper

Candidates' names, addresses and descriptions	Mark your vote in this column

Guidance to Voters

1. This voting paper must be signed, and the full name written on the reverse.
2. Use your single transferable vote by entering '1' against your first preference, and if desired, '2' against your second preference, '3' against your third preference, and so on as far as you wish. The sequence of your preferences is crucial. NO CROSS should be used.
3. You should continue to express preferences for as long as you are able to place successive candidates in order. A later preference is considered only if an earlier preference either has

a surplus above the quota (the minimum number required to guarantee election) or has been excluded because of insufficient support.

4. The numbering of your preferences must be consecutive and given to different candidates. Remember that your making a second or subsequent preference cannot affect the chances of any earlier preference.

5. If you inadvertently spoil your voting paper you may return it to the Presiding Officer who will give you another paper.

6. The voting paper duly completed on the reverse thereof must be delivered (by post or otherwise) to.....................
so as to arrive by no later than ....

(*to be printed on the*   Signature of Voter ....
back of form)   Full name   ....
                          Address   ....

APPENDIX II

Rule 13

GENERAL PROVISIONS RELATING TO PAROCHIAL CHURCH
COUNCILS

Officers of the Council

1. (*a*) The minister of the parish shall be chairman of the
parochial church council (hereinafter referred to as 'the council').

(*b*) A lay member of the council shall be elected as vice-
chairman of the council.

(*c*) During the vacancy of the benefice or when the chairman
is incapacitated by absence or illness or any other cause or
when the minister invites him to do so the vice-chairman of
the council shall act as chairman and have all the powers
vested in the chairman.

(*d*) The council may appoint one of their number to act as
secretary of the council. If no member is appointed so to act
the council shall appoint some other fit person with such
remuneration (if any) as they shall think fit. The secretary
shall have charge of all documents relating to the current
business of the council except that, unless he is the electoral
roll officer, he shall not have charge of the roll. He shall
be responsible for keeping the minutes, shall record all
resolutions passed by the council and shall keep the secretary
of the diocesan synod and deanery synod informed as to his
name and address.

(*e*) The council may appoint one or more of their number
to act as treasurer solely or jointly. Failing such appointment,
the office of treasurer shall be discharged jointly by such of
the churchwardens as are members of the council, or, if there
is only one such churchwarden, by the churchwarden solely.
No remuneration shall be paid to any person in respect of
his appointment as treasurer.

(*f*) The council shall appoint an electoral roll officer, who
may but need not be a member of the council and may be

the secretary and if he is not a member may pay to him such remuneration as it shall think fit. He shall have charge of the roll.

(*g*) If auditors to the council are not appointed by the annual meeting, or if auditors appointed by the annual meeting are unable or unwilling to act, auditors (who shall not be members of the council) shall be appointed by the council. The remuneration (if any) of the auditors shall be paid by the council.

Meetings of Council

2. The council shall hold not less than four meetings in each year. Meetings shall be convened by the chairman and if not more than four meetings are held they shall be at quarterly intervals so far as possible.

Power to Call Meetings

3. The chairman may at any time convene a meeting of the council. If he refuses or neglects to do so within seven days after a requisition for that purpose signed by not less than one-third of the members of the council has been presented to him those members may forthwith convene a meeting.

Notices Relating to Meetings

4. (*a*) Except as provided in paragraph 8 of this Appendix, at least ten clear days before any meeting of the council notice thereof specifying the time and place of the intended meeting and signed by or on behalf of the chairman of the council or the persons convening the meeting shall be posted at or near the principal door of every church, or building licensed for public worship in the parish.

(*b*) Not less than seven days before the meeting a notice thereof specifying the time and place of the meeting signed by or on behalf of the secretary shall be sent to every member of the council. Such notice shall contain the agenda of the meeting including any motion or other business proposed by any member of the council of which notice has been received by the secretary.

(c) If for some good and sufficient reason the chairman, vice-chairman and secretary, or any two of them, consider that a convened meeting should be postponed, notice shall be given to every member of the council specifying a reconvened time and place within fourteen days of the postponed meeting.

Chairman at Meetings

5. Subject to the provisions of rule 18 the chair at a meeting of the council shall be taken—

(a) by the chairman of the council if he is present;
(b) if the chairman of the council is not present, or his office is vacant, by the vice-chairman of the council if he is present;
(c) in the case of a parish in the area of a benefice for which a team ministry is established, by the rector in that ministry if he is present and both the vicar in that ministry who would if he were present be entitled, by virtue of a provision in a pastoral scheme or the bishop's licence, to preside and the vice-chairman of the council are not present:

Provided that at any such meeting the chairman presiding shall, if he thinks it expedient to do so or the meeting so resolves, vacate the chair either generally or for the purpose of any business in which he has a personal interest or for any other particular business.

Should neither the chairman nor, where sub-paragraph (c) above applies, the rector be available to take the chair for any meeting or for any particular item on the agenda during a meeting then a chairman shall be chosen by those members present from among their number and the person so chosen shall preside for that meeting or for that particular item.

Quorum and Agenda

6. No business shall be transacted at any meeting of the council unless at least one-third of the members are present thereat and no business which is not specified in the agenda shall be transacted at any meeting except by the consent of three-quarters of the members present at the meeting.

Order of Business

7. The business of a meeting of the council shall be transacted in the order set forth in the agenda unless the council by resolution otherwise determine.

Short Notice for Emergency Meetings

8. In the case of sudden emergency or other special circumstances requiring immediate action by the council a meeting may be convened by the chairman of the council at not less than three clear days' notice in writing to the members of the council but the quorum for the transaction of any business at such meetings shall be a majority of the then existing members of the council and no business shall be transacted at such meeting except as is specified in the notice convening the meeting.

Place of Meetings

9. The meeting of the council shall be held at such place as the council may direct or in the absence of such direction as the chairman may direct.

Vote of Majority to Decide

10. The business of the council shall be decided by a majority of the members present and voting thereon.

Casting Vote

11. In the case of an equal division of votes the chairman of the meeting shall have a second or casting vote.

Minutes

12. (*a*) The names of the members present at any meeting of the council shall be recorded in the minutes.

(*b*) If one-fifth of the members present and voting on any resolution so require, the minutes shall record the names of the members voting for and against that resolution.

(*c*) Any member of the council shall be entitled to require that the minutes shall contain a record of the manner in which his vote was cast on any resolution.

(*d*) Members of the council shall have access to the minutes of all meetings, but no other person, other than the bishop or the archdeacon or a person authorised by either of them in writing, shall have access to the minutes or part thereof without the authority of the council.

Adjournment

13. Any meeting of the council may adjourn its proceedings to such time and place as may be determined at such meeting.

Standing Committee

14. (*a*) The council shall have a standing committee consisting of not less than five persons. The minister and such of the churchwardens as are members of the council shall be ex-officio members of the standing committee, and the council shall by resolution appoint at least two other members of the standing committee from among its own members and may remove any person so appointed.

(*b*) The standing committee shall have power to transact the business of the council between the meetings thereof subject to any directions given by the council.

Other Committees

15. The council may appoint other committees for the purpose of the various branches of church work in the parish and may include therein persons who are not members of the council. The minister shall be a member of all committees ex-officio.

Validity of Proceedings

16. No proceedings of the council shall be invalidated by any vacancy in the membership of the council or by any defect in the qualification or election of any member thereof.

Interpretation

17. Any question arising on the interpretation of this Appendix shall be referred to the bishop of the diocese and any decision given by him or by any person appointed by him on his behalf shall be final.

APPENDIX 3

Parochial Church Councils (Powers) Measure 1956

1. Definitions.—In this Measure—

'Council' means a parochial church council;

'Diocesan Authority' means the Diocesan Board of Finance or any existing or future body appointed by the Diocesan Conference to act as trustees of diocesan trust property;

'Minister' and 'Parish' have the meanings respectively assigned to them in the Church Representation Rules;

'Relevant date' means the first day of July 1921.

2. General functions of council.—

(1) It shall be the duty of the incumbent and the parochial church council to consult together on matters of general concern and importance to the parish.

(2) The functions of parochial church councils shall include—

- (*a*) co-operation with the incumbent in promoting in the parish the whole mission of the Church, pastoral, evangelistic, social and ecumenical;
- (*b*) the consideration and discussions of matters concerning the Church of England or any other matters of religious or public interest, but not the declaration of the doctrine of the Church on any question;
- (*c*) making known and putting into effect any provision made by the diocesan synod or the deanery synod, but without prejudice to the powers of the council on any particular matter;

(*d*) giving advice to the diocesan synod and the deanery synod on any matter referred to the council;

(*e*) raising such matters as the council consider appropriate with the diocesan synod or deanery synod.

(3) In the exercise of its functions the parochial church council shall take into consideration any expression of opinion by any parochial church meeting.

3. Council to be a body corporate.—Every council shall be a body corporate by the name of the parochial church council of the parish for which it is appointed and shall have perpetual succession. Any act of the council may be signified by an instrument executed pursuant to a resolution of the council and under the hands or if an instrument under seal is required under the hands and seals of the chairman presiding and two other members of the council present at the meeting at which such resolution is passed.

4. Powers vested in council as successor to certain other bodies.—(1) Subject to the provisions of any Act or Measure passed after the relevant date and to anything lawfully done under such provisions, the council of every parish shall have—

(i) The like power duties and liabilities as, immediately before the relevant date, the vestry of such parish had with respect to the affairs of the church except as regards the election of churchwardens and sidesmen and as regards the administration of ecclesiastical charities but including the power of presentation to the benefice of such parish if the right to present thereto was vested in or in trust for the parishioners and the power of making any voluntary church rate.

(ii) The like powers duties and liabilities as, immediately before the relevant date, the churchwardens of such parish had with respect to—

(*a*) The financial affairs of the church including the collection and administration of all moneys raised for church purposes and the keeping of accounts in relation to such affairs and moneys;

(*b*) The care maintenance preservation and insurance of the fabric of the church and the goods and ornaments thereof;

(*c*) The care and maintenance of any churchyard (open or closed), and the power of giving a certificate under the provisions of section eighteen of the Burial Act 1855, with the like powers as, immediately before the relevant date, were possessed by the churchwardens to recover the cost of maintaining a closed churchyard:

Provided that nothing herein contained shall affect the property of the churchwardens in the goods and ornaments of the church or their powers duties and liabilities with respect to visitations.

(iii) The like powers duties and liabilities as, immediately before the relevant date, were possessed by the church trustees (if any) for the parish appointed under the Compulsory Church Rate Abolition Act 1868.

(2) All enactments in any Act whether general or local or personal relating to any powers duties or liabilities transferred to the council from the vestry churchwardens or church trustees as the case may be shall subject to the provisions of this Measure and so far as circumstances admit be construed as if any reference therein to the vestry or the churchwardens or church trustees referred to the council to which such duties powers or liabilities have been transferred and the said enactments shall be construed with such modifications as may be necessary for carrying this Measure into effect.

(3) Where any property is applicable to purposes connected with any such powers duties or liabilities as aforesaid, any deed or instrument which could be or could have been made or executed in relation to such property by a vestry, or by churchwardens or church trustees, may be made or executed by the council of the parish concerned.

(4) This Measure shall not affect any enactment in any private

or local Act of Parliament under the authority of which church rates may be made or levied in lieu of or in consideration of the extinguishment or of the appropriation to any other purpose of any tithes customary payments or other property or charge upon property which tithes payments property or charge previously to the passing of such Act had been appropriated by law to ecclesiastical purposes or in consideration of the abolition of tithes in any place or upon any contract made or for good or valuable consideration given and every such enactment shall continue in force in the same manner as if this Measure had not been passed.

For the purposes of this subsection 'ecclesiastical purposes' shall mean the building rebuilding enlargement and repair of any church and any purpose to which by common or ecclesiastical law a church rate is applicable or any of such purposes.

5. Holding of property for ecclesiastical purposes: educational schemes.—(1) Subject to the provisions of this Measure, the council of every parish shall have power to acquire (whether by way of gift or otherwise) any property real or personal—

(*a*) For any ecclesiastical purpose affecting the parish or any part thereof;

(*b*) For any purpose in connection with schemes (hereinafter called 'educational schemes') for providing facilities for the spiritual moral and physical training of persons residing in or near the parish.

(2) Subject to the provisions of this Measure and of the general law and to the provisions of any trusts affecting any such property, the council shall have power to manage, administer and dispose of any property acquired under this section.

(3) A council shall have power, in connection with any educational scheme, to constitute or participate in the constitution of a body of managers or trustees or a managing committee consisting either wholly or partly of persons

appointed by the council, and may confer on any such body or committee such functions in regard to the implementation of the scheme, and such functions relating to property held for the purposes of the scheme, as the council thinks expedient.

(4) The powers of a council with respect to educational schemes shall be exercised subject to and in accordance with the terms of any undertaking which may have been given by the council to the Minister of Education[1] or to any local authority in connection with any financial or other assistance given by the Minister[1] or the authority in relation to the scheme.

(5) A council shall not exercise any of its powers in relation to educational schemes without the consent of the diocesan education committee of the diocese, and any such consent may be given upon such terms and conditions as the committee considers appropriate in all the circumstances of the case.

In this subsection the expression 'diocesan education committee' includes any body of persons whether incorporated or not for the time being having the functions of such a committee by virtue of the Diocesan Education Committees Measure 1955, and any orders made thereunder.

6. Supplementary provisions relating to certain property.—(1) After the commencement of this Measure, a council shall not acquire any interest in land (other than a short lease as hereinafter defined) or in any personal property to be held on permanent trusts, without the consent of the diocesan authority.

(2) Where, at or after the commencement of this Measure, a council holds or acquires an interest in land (other than a short lease as hereinafter defined) or any interest in personal property to be held on permanent trusts, such interest shall be vested in the diocesan authority subject to all trusts, debts and liabilities affecting the same, and all persons concerned shall make or concur in making such transfers (if any) as are requisite for giving effect to the provisions of this subsection.

(3) Where any property is vested in the diocesan authority

1 Now the Secretary of State for Education and Science.

pursuant to subsection (2) of this section, the council shall not sell, lease, let, exchange, charge or take any legal proceedings with respect to the property without the consent of the authority; but save as aforesaid, nothing in this section shall affect the powers of the council in relation to the management, administration or disposition of any such property.

(4) Where any property is vested in the diocesan authority pursuant to subsection (2) of this section, the council shall keep the authority indemnified in respect of:

(a) all liabilities subject to which the property is vested in the authority or which may thereafter be incident to the property;

(b) all rates, taxes, insurance premiums and other outgoings of whatever nature which may from time to time be payable in respect of the property;

(c) all costs, charges and expenses incurred by the authority in relation to the acquisition or insurance of the property or as trustee thereof;

(d) all costs, proceedings, claims and demands in respect of any of the matters hereinbefore mentioned.

(5) The consents required by subsection (3) of this section are additional to any other consents required by law, either from the Charity Commissioners or the Minister of Education[1] or otherwise.

(6) In this section the expression 'short lease' means a lease for a term not exceeding one year, and includes any tenancy from week to week, from month to month, from quarter to quarter, or from year to year.

(7) Any question as to whether personal property is to be held on permanent trusts shall be determined for the purposes of this section by a person appointed by the bishop.

7. Miscellaneous powers of council.—The council of every parish shall have the following powers in addition to any powers conferred by the Constitution or otherwise by this Measure:—

1 See note 1 on p 219, above.

(i) Power to frame an annual budget of moneys required for the maintenance of the work of the Church in the parish and otherwise and to take such steps as they think necessary for the raising collecting and allocating of such moneys;

(ii) Power to make levy and collect a voluntary church rate for any purpose connected with the affairs of the church including the administrative expenses of the council and the costs of any legal proceedings;

(iii) Power jointly with the minister to appoint and dismiss the parish clerk and sexton or any persons performing or assisting to perform the duties of parish clerk or sexton and to determine their salaries and the conditions of the tenure of their offices or of their employment but subject to the rights of any persons holding the said offices at the [appointed day];[1]

(iv) Power jointly with the minister to determine the objects to which all moneys to be given or collected in church shall be allocated . . .;[2]

(v) Power to make representations to the bishop with regard to any matter affecting the welfare of the church in the parish.

8. Accounts of the council.—(1) Every council shall furnish to the annual parochial church meeting the audited accounts of the council for the year ending on 31 December immediately preceding the meeting and an audited statement of the funds and property, if any, remaining in the hands of the council at that date.

(2) At least seven days before the annual parochial church meeting, the council shall cause a copy of the said audited accounts and a copy of the said statement to be affixed at or

1 'Relevant date' was clearly intended.
2 The words 'subject to the directions contained in the Book of Common Prayer as to the disposal of money given at the offertory' were repealed by the Church of England (Legal Aid and Miscellaneous Provisions) Measure 1988, ss 13, 14 (2), Sch 3.

near the principal door of the parish church as required by
paragraph (2) of Rule 8 of the Church Representation Rules.

(3) The accounts and statement shall be submitted to the
meeting for approval, and, if approved, they shall be signed by
the chairman of the meeting who shall then deliver them to the
council for publication, and the council shall forthwith cause
them to be published in the manner provided by paragraph (3)
of Rule 8 of the Church Representation Rules.

(4) The accounts of all trusts administered by the council
shall be laid before the diocesan authority annually.

9. Powers of bishop.—(1) The bishop may subject to the
provisions of this Measure and the Constitution make rules for
carrying this Measure into effect within the diocese.

(2) If any act required by this Measure to be done by any
person is not done within such time as the bishop may consider
reasonable it may be done by or under the authority of the
bishop.

(3) In the event of a council and a minister being unable to
agree as to any matter in which their agreement or joint action
is required under the provisions of this Measure, such matter
shall be dealt with or determined in such manner as the bishop
may direct.

(4) During a vacancy in a diocesan see the powers conferred
upon the bishop by this section may be exercised by the guardian
of the spiritualities.

10. Short title, commencement, extent and repeals.—(1)
This Measure may be cited as the Parochial Church Councils
(Powers) Measure 1956.

(2) This Measure shall come into operation on the second
day of January 1957.

(3) This Measure shall extend to the whole of the Provinces
of Canterbury and York except the Channel Islands and the Isle
of Man:

Provided that, if an Act of Tynwald so provides, this Measure
shall extend to the Isle of Man subject to such modifications, if
any, as may be specified in such Act of Tynwald.

(4) The Parochial Church Councils (Powers) Measure 1921, and the Parochial Church Councils (Powers) (Amendment) Measure 1949, are hereby repealed.

APPENDIX 4

Churchwardens (Appointment and Resignation) Measure 1964[1]

1. Number and qualifications of churchwardens.—(1) Subject to the provisions of this Measure there shall be two churchwardens of every parish.

(2) The churchwardens of every parish shall be chosen from persons who are resident in the parish or whose names are on the church electoral roll of the parish.

(3) Such persons shall be actual communicant members of the Church of England except where the bishop shall otherwise permit and of twenty-one years of age and upwards.

(4) No person shall be chosen as a churchwarden unless he has signified his consent to serve.

2. Time and manner of choosing churchwardens.—(1) The churchwardens of a parish shall be chosen annually not later than 30 April in each year.

(2) Subject to the provisions of this Measure the churchwardens of a parish shall be chosen by the joint consent of the minister of the parish and a meeting of the parishioners if it may be; such joint consent shall be deemed to have been signified:—

(a) if any motion stating the names of the persons to be chosen as churchwardens or the name of either of them shall be declared by the person presiding over the meeting to have been carried; and

(b) if in respect of any such motion the minister shall have announced his consent to the choice of the person or

1 As amended by the Church Representation Rules.

persons named therein either before the putting of the motion to the meeting or immediately upon the declaration of the result thereof:

Provided that no person shall be deemed to have been chosen as a churchwarden under the provisions of this subsection unless both churchwardens have been so chosen.

(3) If the minister of the parish and the meeting of the parishioners cannot agree on the choice of both churchwardens by joint consent as provided in the foregoing subsection or if after due opportunity has been given no motions or insufficient motions have been moved in accordance with the provisions of that subsection then one churchwarden shall be appointed by the minister and the other shall then be elected by the meeting of the parishioners.

(4) During any period when there is no minister both the churchwardens shall be elected by the meeting of the parishioners.

(5) A person may be chosen to fill a casual vacancy among the churchwardens at any time.

(6) Any person chosen to fill a casual vacancy shall be chosen in the same manner as was the churchwarden in whose place he is appointed.

3. Meeting of the parishioners—(1) A joint meeting of:—

(a) the persons whose names are entered on the church electoral roll of the parish; and

(b) the persons resident in the parish whose names are entered on a register of local government electors by reason of such residence

shall be deemed to be a meeting of the parishioners for the purposes of this Measure.

(2) The meeting of the parishioners shall be convened by the minister or the churchwardens of the parish by a notice signed by the minister or a churchwarden.

(3) The notice shall state the place, day and hour at which the meeting of the parishioners is to be held.

(4) The notice shall be affixed on or near to the principal door of the parish church and of every other building licensed for public worship in the parish for a period including the last two Sundays before the meeting.

(5) The minister, if present, or, if he is not present, a chairman chosen by the meeting of the parishioners, shall preside thereat.

(6) In case of an equal division of votes the chairman of the meeting of the parishioners shall have a casting vote.[1]

(7) The meeting of the parishioners shall have power to adjourn, and to determine its own rules of procedure.

(8) A person appointed by the meeting of the parishioners shall act as clerk of the meeting and shall record the minutes thereof.

[*Sections* **4, 5** *and* **6** *repealed by the Church Representation Rules.*]

7. Admission of churchwardens.—(1) At a time and place to be appointed by the Ordinary each person chosen for the office of churchwarden shall appear before the Ordinary, or his substitute duly appointed, and be admitted to the office of churchwarden after subscribing the declaration that he will faithfully and diligently perform the duties of his office, and making the same in the presence of the Ordinary or his substitute. No person chosen for the office of churchwarden shall become churchwarden until such time as he shall have been admitted to office in accordance with the provisions of this section.

(2) Subject to the provisions of this Measure the churchwardens so chosen and admitted as aforesaid shall continue in their office until they, or others as their successors, be admitted in like manner before the Ordinary.

8. Resignation of churchwardens.—(1) If a churchwarden

1 Not applicable to elections of churchwardens (rule 11 (2) of Church Representation Rules).

wishes to resign his office he may, with the consent in writing of the minister and any other churchwarden of the parish, resign his office by an instrument in writing addressed to the bishop, and if the bishop accepts his resignation his office shall forthwith be vacated.

(2) Subject to the provisions of this section a churchwarden shall not be entitled to resign his office.

9. Vacation of office.—The office of churchwarden shall be vacated if the churchwarden is not resident in the parish and if his name is not on the church electoral roll of the parish.

10. Guild Churches.—(1) In the case of every church in the City of London designated and established as a Guild Church under the City of London (Guild Churches) Acts 1952 and 1960, the churchwardens shall, notwithstanding anything to the contrary contained in those Acts, be actual communicant members of the Church of England except where the bishop shall otherwise permit.

(2) Subject to the provisions of subsection (1) of this section, nothing in this Measure shall apply to the churchwardens of any church designated and established as a Guild Church under the City of London (Guild Churches) Acts 1952 and 1960.

11. Special provisions.—(1) In the carrying out of this Measure in any diocese the bishop of such diocese shall have power:—

   (*a*) to make provision for any matter not herein provided for;

   (*b*) to appoint a person to do any act in respect of which there has been any neglect or default on the part of any person or body charged with any duty under this Measure;

   (*c*) so far as may be necessary for the purpose of giving effect to the intentions of this Measure, to extend or alter the time for holding any meeting or election or to modify the procedure laid down by this Measure in connection therewith;

(*d*) in any case in which there has been no valid choice, to direct a fresh choice to be made, and to give such directions in connection therewith as he may think necessary; and

(*e*) in any case in which any difficulty arises, to give any directions which he may consider expedient for the purpose of removing the difficulty.

(2) The powers of the bishop under this section shall not enable him to validate anything that was invalid at the time it was done.

(3) [*Repealed by the Church Representation Rules.*]

(4) During a vacancy in a diocesan see the powers by this section conferred upon a bishop of the diocese shall be exercisable by the guardian of the spiritualities.

12. Savings.—(1) Subject to the provisions of section ten of this Measure, nothing in this Measure shall be deemed to amend, repeal or affect any local Act or any scheme made under any enactment affecting the churchwardens of a parish:

Provided that for the purposes of this Measure the Parish of Manchester Division Act 1850 shall be deemed to be a general Act.

(2) In the case of any parish where there is an existing custom which regulates the number of churchwardens or the manner in which the churchwardens are chosen, nothing in this Measure shall affect that custom:

Provided that in the case of any parish where in accordance with that custom any churchwarden is chosen by the vestry of that parish either alone or jointly with any other person or persons that churchwarden shall be chosen by the meeting of the parishioners, either alone or jointly with the other person or persons, as the case may be.

(3) Nothing in this Measure shall affect a churchwarden in office before the passing of this Measure during the period for which he was chosen.

(4) Nothing in this Measure shall be deemed to authorise the choice of any person as churchwarden who under the existing law is disqualified from being chosen for that office.

13. Interpretation.—In this Measure, except in so far as the context otherwise requires:—

   'existing custom' means a custom existing at the commencement of this Measure which has continued for a period including the last forty years before its commencement;
   'Rules for the Representation of the Laity' means the Rules for the Representation of the Laity contained in the Schedule to the Representation of the Laity Measure 1956;
   'actual communicant member', 'minister', 'parish' and 'public worship' have the same meanings respectively as those assigned to those expressions in Rule 1 of the Rules for the Representation of the Laity.[1]

14. Repeal.—Section twelve of the New Parishes Measure 1943, and Rule 10 of the Rules for the Representation of the Laity are hereby repealed.

15. Short title, extent and commencement.—(1) This Measure may be cited as the Churchwardens (Appointment and Registration) Measure 1964.

(2) This Measure shall extend to the whole of the provinces of Canterbury and York except for the Channel Islands and the Isle of Man:

Provided that—

   (*a*) this Measure may be applied to the Channel Islands as defined in the Channel Islands (Church Legislation) Measures 1931 and 1957 or either of them in accordance with those Measures;
   (*b*) if an Act of Tynwald so provides this Measure shall extend to the Isle of Man subject to such modifications, if any, as may be specified in such Act of Tynwald.

1 See now rule 44 of the Church Representation Rules.

(3) This Measure shall come into force on the first day of January next after the date on which it receives the Royal Assent.

Table of Enactments referred to in this Measure

Short Title	Session and Chapter
Parish of Manchester Division Act 1850	13 & 14 Vict c xli
Channel Islands (Church Legislation) Measure 1931	21 & 22 Geo 5 No 4
New Parishes Measure 1942	6 & 7 Geo 6 No 1
City of London (Guild Churches) Act 1952	15 & 16 Geo 6 & 1 Eliz 2 c xxxviii
Representation of the Laity Measure 1956	4 & 5 Eliz 2 No 2
Channel Islands (Church Legislation) Measure 1931 (Amendment) Measure 1957	5 & 6 Eliz 2 No 1
City of London (Guild Churches) Act 1960	8 & 9 Eliz 2 c xxx

Patronage (Benefices) Measure 1986, sections 11 and 12

11. Requirements as to meetings of parochial church council.—(1) Before the expiration of the period of four weeks beginning with the date on which the notice under section 7 (4) of this Measure is sent to the secretary of the parochial church council, one or more meetings of that council shall be held for the purposes of—

- (*a*) preparing a statement describing the conditions, needs and traditions of the parish;
- (*b*) appointing two lay members of the council to act as representatives of the council in connection with the selection of an incumbent;
- (*c*) deciding whether to request the registered patron to consider advertising the vacancy;
- (*d*) deciding whether to request a meeting under section 12 of this Measure; and
- (*e*) deciding whether to request a statement in writing from the bishop describing in relation to the benefice the needs of the diocese and the wider interests of the Church.

(2) A meeting of the parochial church council for which subsection (1) above provides shall be convened by the secretary thereof, and no member of that council who is—

- (*a*) the outgoing incumbent or the wife of the outgoing incumbent, or

(b) the registered patron, or

(c) the representative of the registered patron,

shall attend that meeting.

(3) None of the following members of the parochial church council, that is to say—

(a) any person mentioned in subsection (2) above, and

(b) any deaconess or lay worker licensed to the parish,

shall be qualified for appointment under subsection (1) (b) above.

(4) If before the vacancy in the benefice is filled any person appointed under subsection (1) (b) above dies or becomes unable for any reason to act as the representative of, or ceases to be a member of, the council by which he was appointed, then, except where he ceases to be such a member and the council decides that he shall continue to act as its representative, his appointment shall be deemed to have been revoked and the council shall appoint another lay member of the council (not being a member disqualified under subsection (3) above) to act in his place for the remainder of the proceedings under this Part of this Measure.

(5) If a parochial church council holds a meeting under subsection (1) above but does not appoint any representatives at that meeting, then, subject to subsection (6) below, two churchwardens who are members of that council (or, if there are more than two churchwardens who are members of the council, two churchwardens chosen by all the churchwardens who are members) shall act as representatives of the council in connection with the selection of an incumbent.

(6) A churchwarden who is the registered patron of a

benefice shall not be qualified under subsection (5) above to act as a representative of the parochial church council or to choose any other churchwarden so to act, and in any case where there is only one churchwarden qualified to act as such a representative that churchwarden may act as the sole representative of that council in connection with the selection of the incumbent.

(7) Any representative of the parochial church council appointed under subsection (1) or (4) above and any churchwarden acting as such a representative by virtue of subsection (5) or (6) above is in this Part of this Measure referred to as a 'parish representative', and where a churchwarden is entitled to act as the sole parish representative any reference in this Part to the parish representatives shall be construed as a reference to that churchwarden.

(8) A copy of the statement prepared under subsection (1) (*a*) above together with the names and addresses of the parish representatives shall, as soon as practicable after the holding of the meeting under that subsection, be sent by the secretary of the parochial church council to the registered patron and, unless the bishop is the registered patron, to the bishop.

12. Joint meeting of parochial church council with bishop and patron.—(1) Where a request for a meeting under this section is made—

(*a*) by a notice sent by the registered patron or the bishop to the secretary of the parochial church council, or

(*b*) by a resolution of the parochial church council, passed at a meeting held under section 11 of this Measure, a joint meeting of the parochial church council with the registered patron and (if the bishop is not the registered patron) the bishop shall be held for the purpose of enabling those present at the meeting to exchange views on the statement prepared under section 11 (1) (*a*) of this Measure (needs of the parish) and the statement presented under subsection (2) below (needs of the diocese).

(2) At any meeting held under this section the bishop shall present either orally or, if a request for a statement in writing has been made by the registered patron or the parochial church council, in writing a statement describing in relation to the benefice the needs of the diocese and the wider interests of the Church.

(3) Any notice given under subsection (1) (*a*) above shall be of no effect unless it is sent to the secretary of the parochial church council not later than ten days after a copy of the statement prepared under subsection (1) (*a*) of section 11 of this Measure is received by the persons mentioned in subsection (8) of that section.

(4) The outgoing incumbent and the wife of the outgoing incumbent shall not be entitled to attend a meeting held under this section.

(5) A meeting requested under this section shall be held before the expiration of the period of six weeks beginning with the date on which the request for the meeting was first made (whether by the sending of a notice as mentioned in subsection (1) (*a*) above or by the passing of a resolution as mentioned in subsection (1) (*b*) above), and at least fourteen days' notice (unless a shorter period is agreed by all the persons concerned) of the time and place at which the meeting is to be held shall be given by the secretary of the parochial church council to the

registered patron, the bishop (if he is not the registered patron) and the members of the parochial church council.

(6) If either the registered patron or the bishop is unable to attend a meeting held under this section, he shall appoint some other person to attend on his behalf.

(7) The chairman of any meeting held under this section shall be such person as the persons who are entitled to attend and are present at the meeting may determine.

(8) No meeting requested under this section shall be treated for the purposes of this Measure as having been held unless there were present at the meeting—

- (*a*) the bishop or the person appointed by the bishop to attend on his behalf, and
- (*b*) the registered patron or the person appointed by the patron to attend on his behalf, and
- (*c*) at least one third of the members of the parochial church council who were entitled to attend.

(9) The secretary of the parochial church council shall invite both the rural dean of the deanery in which the parish is (unless he is the outgoing incumbent) and the lay chairman of the deanery synod of that deanery to attend a meeting held under this section.

APPENDIX 6

Parochial Fees Order 1988

(SI 1988/1327)

SCHEDULE TABLE OF PAROCHIAL FEES PART I

	Col 1 Fee payable to Incumbent	Col 2 Fee payable to Parochial Church Council	Col 3 TOTAL FEES PAYABLE	Col 4 Fee payable to Clerk (See PART II para 1 below)	Col 5 Fee payable to Sexton (See PART II para 1 below)
	£	£	£	£	£
BAPTISMS					
Certificate issued at time of baptism	2.50	—	**2.50**	—	—
Short certificate of baptism given under section 2 Baptismal Registers Measure 1961	1.50	—	**1.50**	—	—
MARRIAGES					
Publication of banns of marriage	3.50	1.50	**5.00**	1.50	—
Certificate of banns issued at time of publication	2.50	—	**2.50**	—	—
Marriage service	19.50	19.50	**39.00**	10.00	—
FUNERALS AND BURIALS					
A. Service in church					
For funeral service in church	12.50	8.50	**21.00**	4.00	4.00

	Col 1 Fee payable to Incumbent	Col 2 Fee payable to Parochial Church Council	Col 3 TOTAL FEES PAYABLE	Col 4 Fee payable to Clerk (See PART II para 1 below)	Col 5 Fee payable to Sexton (See PART II para 1 below)
Burial in churchyard immediately after service in church	—	21.00	21.00	—	—
Burial in consecrated part of cemetery immediately after service in church	—	—	NIL	—	—
Burial in churchyard on separate occasion	7.00	21.00	28.00	—	—
Burial in consecrated part of cemetery on separate occasion	7.00	—	7.00	—	—
B. *No service in church* Service in consecrated part of cemetery	21.00	—	21.00	—	—
Burial in churchyard	7.00	21.00	28.00	4.00	4.00
C. *Certificate issued at time of burial*	2.50	—	2.50	—	—

MONUMENTS IN CHURCHYARDS

Erected with consent of incumbent under Chancellor's general directions—

exceeding 12″ × 8″ × 8″ (approx. 300mm × 200mm × 200mm)(*)	4.50	6.00	**10.50**	1.00
Tablet, erected horizontally or vertically and not exceeding 21″ × 21″ (approx. 525mm × 525mm), commemorating person cremated(*)	9.50	9.50	**19.00**	2.50
Any other monument(*)	21.50	23.00	**44.50**	4.50
Additional inscription on existing monument	10.00	—	**10.00**	

SEARCHES IN CHURCH REGISTERS, ETC

Searching registers of marriages for period before 1837				
(for up to one hour)	2.50	2.00	**4.50**	
(for each subsequent hour or part of an hour)	2.00	1.00	**3.00**	
Searching registers of baptisms or burials (including provision of one copy of any entry therein)				
(for up to one hour)	2.50	2.00	**4.50**	

	Col 1 Fee payable to Incumbent	Col 2 Fee payable to Parochial Church Council	Col 3 TOTAL FEES PAYABLE	Col 4 Fee payable to Clerk (See PART II para 1 below)	Col 5 Fee payable to Sexton (See PART II para 1 below)
(for each subsequent hour or part of an hour)	2.00	1.00	**3.00**	—	—
Each additional copy of an entry in a register of baptisms or burials	2.50	2.00	**4.50**	—	—
Inspection of instrument of apportionment or agreement for exchange of land for tithes deposited under Tithe Act 1836	1.50	—	**1.50**	—	—
Furnishing copies of above (for every 72 words)	1.50	—	**1.50**	—	—

(*)See Part II para 4.

PART II

1. *Clerks and Sextons*
In certain parishes there will still be a person who

(i) was employed in a parish immediately before 1st January 1977 (the date on which the Parochial Fees Order 1976 came into operation) as a parish clerk or sexton; or

(ii) under the terms of his or her employment carried out the duties of a clerk or sexton and was entitled to fees payable for such duties.

That person is, in relation to that parish, entitled to be paid the sum specified in column 4 for performing a clerk's duties or that in column 5 for performing a sexton's duties; and the sum shown in column 2 as payable to the parochial church council shall be reduced accordingly.

Where there is no person entitled as above to the sum specified in column 4 or column 5 (or either of them) such sum or sums are payable to the incumbent, if he was incumbent of the parish immediately before 1st January 1977; and the sum shown in column 2 as payable to the parochial church council shall be reduced accordingly.

2. *Burial of still-born infant*
No fee is payable in respect of the burial of a still-born infant, or for the funeral or burial of an infant dying within the neo-natal period of 28 days after birth.

3. *Cremated remains in churches or closed churchyards*
Where cremated remains are buried in or under a church or in a closed churchyard, the fees payable to the incumbent and the parochial church council are:

(ii) where burial is authorised by a general faculty, the same as those laid down in Part I of this table for burial in a churchyard;

(ii) where burial is authorised by a particular faculty, such sums as may be determined by the chancellor.

4. *Monuments in churchyards*

The fees marked (*) include fees for the original inscription. Where a monument in a churchyard is erected or an additional inscription on a monument is made **under the authority of a particular faculty** the fees payable to the incumbent and the parochial church council or either of them shall be such sums as may be determined by the chancellor who shall specify the persons entitled to receive them.

5. *Monuments in churches*

Where a faculty is granted in connection with the erection of a monument or tablet in a church or any additional inscription thereon, the fees payable to the incumbent and the parochial church council or either of them shall be determined by the chancellor who shall specify the persons entitled to receive them.

6. *The incumbent's fees*

The incumbent may direct either generally or in particular cases that any fee which would otherwise be payable to him shall be payable to the minister performing the service or duty.

7. *Reservation of grave space: vaults*

Payment of any of the fees prescribed by this table does not confer any right to construct a new vault or an exclusive right to a grave or vault. Where a faculty is granted conferring rights for a period specified in the faculty, the fees payable to the incumbent and the parochial church council or either of them shall be determined by the chancellor who shall specify the persons entitled to receive them.

Index

Service—*continued*
baptism, 58–60
Bible, versions of, 50
Book of Common Prayer, 47
burial, 73–8
collection, 51
General Synod powers, 4, 46–9
guild churches, 47*n*
Holy Communion, 55–7
incumbent's duty to provide, 46
interruption of, 106
irregular manner, conducted in, 106
lay persons, taken by, 51
lessons, 49
marriage, 60–73
parochial church council, 38
Psalter, Revised, 50
register book of, 94
right to attend, 4
Royal Family, prayers for, 48, 49
rules for regulation of, 51
statute law, 46
variations in, 50
Worship and Doctrine Measure, 46
Service book
requirement to provide, 94
Sexton, 81–3
appointment and dismissal, 82, 221
duties, 81, 82
female, 82
office may be for life, 82
salary and fees, 82, 89, 241
Ship, banns on board, 67*n*
Sick
infant, baptism of, 59
visitation, 56
Sidesmen
appointment, 42, 45, 216
duties, 44–5
election of, 35
number, 45
Sittings in church
allocation of, 101
chancel, seats in, 102
churchwardens' duties, 101, 102
family pews, 103

Sittings in church—*continued*
payment for seating, 102
perturbation of seat, abolition of action for, 102, 128
poor, free seats for, 104
prescription, entitlement by, 103
private chapels, 103
repair, liability for, 103
right to
appurtenant to dwelling-house, 103
incumbent, 103
parishioner, 101
perpetual right to occupy, 103
rector, 103
seating, requirement to provide, 94
statutory provisions, 103, 104
Statute law, 1–2
Still-born child, burial of, 75, 241
Suicides, burial of, 75–6
Surplices, requirement to provide, 94
Surrogate, 67
Suspension, 126–7
Synodical Government Measure, 7–16
Synods. *See* DEANERY SYNOD: DIOCESAN SYNOD; GENERAL SYNOD

Team ministry
establishment of, 17, 20
meetings, 21
parochial church meeting, 143–4
schemes for creation, 20
team parochial church councils, 36, 152–3, 158–9
vicar, status of, 19
Tithes, incumbent's claim to, 17*n*
Tombstones. *See* MONUMENTS AND TOMBSTONES
Trade or occupation, clergy licensed to engage in, 38
Trees, churchyard, in, 108
Trespass, church or churchyard, in, 104, 108, 110